Ten Steps TO A Federal Job®

THE STARS ARE LINED UP FOR
Military Spouses

By Kathryn Troutman

Federal Jobs for Military Spouses
through USAJOBS, Program S, NAF
and Excepted Service

THE
RESUME PLACE
BUILDING CAREERS IN THE US GOVERNMENT

The Resume Place, Inc.

Federal Career Publishers

P.O. Box 21275, Catonsville, MD 21228
Phone: 888-480-8265
www.resume-place.com
Email: govtraining@resume-place.com

Printed in the United States of America
The Stars Are Lined Up for Military Spouses: ISBN-13: 978-0-9861421-8-5 | ISBN-10: 986142182
Copyright © 2017 by Kathryn Troutman

Certified Federal Career Coach®, Certified Federal Job Search Trainer®, The Resume Place®, and Ten Steps to a Federal Job® are trademarks of The Resume Place, Inc.

We have been careful to provide accurate federal job search information in this book, but it is possible that errors and omissions may have been introduced.

Sample resumes are real but fictionalized. All federal applicants have given permission for their resumes to be used as samples for this publication. Privacy policy is strictly enforced.

PUBLICATION TEAM
Cover Design: Brian Moore
Interior Page Design: Brian Moore and Paulina Chen
Developmental Editing and Interior Page Layout: Paulina Chen
Human Resources Editing: Ellen Lazarus
Proofing and Copyediting: Pam Sikora
Program S Consultants: Gloria Garza, Gina Moore, Bobbi Rossiter, and Rose Holland
Military Spouse Program S Contributors:
Bobbi Rossiter, Jennifer Primus, Natalie Skelton, Susanne James, and Kerri-Anne Grant
Index: Pilar Wyman

Table of Contents

Introduction by Kathryn Troutman 5

Part 1: Federal Employment Information 7

   USAJOBS.gov 9

   Federal Career Benefits 10

   Federal Salaries 11

   Work-Life Benefits 12

   Retirement and Insurance 13

   GS Salary Table 14

   Classification Standards 15

   What Is a Competitive Federal Resume? 16

   The Best Federal Resume Format 17

   What to Include in Your Federal Resume 18

Part 2: The Stars Are Lined Up for Military Spouses: Program S 19

   Eligibility: Does Not Expire 21

   Star 1: Who Qualifies for Program S? 22

      E.O. 13473 Requirements 23

      Which Federal Jobs Qualify? 24

      Sample PCS Orders 25

   Star 2: Write Your Federal Resume 26

      Case Study: Bobbi Robbins 27

      Bobbi Robbins' Program S Resume 28

      Keywords for Option Codes 33

   Star 3: Find Your Documents 36

      Sample Welcome Email from OCHR-San Diego, CA 37

   Star 4: Set Up Your Program S Meeting 38

      Program S HRO Contacts 39

      Eligibility Questionnaire 40

   Star 5: Improve Your Program S Registry 41

   Star 6: PPP Match Notification 42

   Star 7: Apply for Jobs on USAJOBS 43

      Apply for Other Jobs—Not Just DOD Jobs 44

   Star 8: Save a Search for Job Matches 45

   Star 9: Follow Up on USAJOBS 46

   Star 10: Get Best Qualified 47

PPP-S Narrative Resumes: Three Before and After Case Studies 48

    After Resume: Jennifer Morris 49

    Before Resume: Jennifer Morris 53

    After Resume: Lori-Anne Romeo 56

    Before Resume: Lori-Anne Romeo 62

    After Resume: Natalie Richardson 67

    Before Resume: Natalie Richardson 70

Part 3: Competitive and Merit Promotion Positions on USAJOBS 71

    What Are Competitive and Merit Promotion Positions? 72

    Sample Builder Federal Resume in the Outline Format 74

    USAJOBS Resume Builder: Store Up to Five Resumes 77

    USAJOBS Tips 78

Part 4: Excepted Service Federal Jobs 79

    What is the Difference Between Competitive and Excepted Service? 80

    Examples of Excepted Service Positions 81

    Sample Job Block for Excepted Service Resume: Social Worker 82

Part 5: NAF Jobs 83

    What is an NAF Job? 84

    NAF Employment Benefits 86

    Writing Your NAF Resume 87

    NAF Resume Sample 89

Part 6: Derived Preference for Military Spouses 91

    What is Derived Preference? 92

    Successful Application with Derived Preference: Results Email from DOD 93

    After Resume: Derived Preference 94

    Before Resume: Derived Preference 98

Appendix: PPP Handbook 100

Index

About the Author

Introduction

For decades, I've been dedicated to helping veterans and military spouses find meaningful employment. My passion for helping military spouses came, in part, from my own life experience. I was a military spouse myself, married to a Sailor. We were stationed near Vallejo, California.

I did not take advantage of anything on the base, except for the medical facilities and the Navy Exchange. In those days, support for military spouses was more limited. I didn't look for opportunities on base because I was just 19 years old and intimidated by the base and its complexities. To help support our family, I held two jobs. I worked for State Farm as a secretary/claims representative and sold Avon in the evenings door-to-door. I kept busy with work and didn't have any kind of military life on the base.

Today's military is more focused on spouses like me. The U.S. government now recognizes how important it is to support all members of military families through development programs and hiring opportunities. Unfortunately, these opportunities can be difficult to access and understand. As I travel around the world, from military base to military base, spouses often tell me they are confused and daunted by the multiple spouse employment programs available to them. At the same time, they are eager and excited to find jobs.

MILITARY SPOUSES DESERVE A CAREER! Military spouses want and deserve their own careers if they choose to work while relocating every few years with their spouse. Finding permanent, career positions every two to four years is more than difficult in the private sector.

But the one employer who has positions and careers at every military base in the world is the U.S. government, and the government is the largest employer in the world!

The curriculum and resources in this book will empower you to get brave and find a great career that you can take with you at each posting. Why not give a government job a real try? Once you get your first government position, you can apply to another similar position at your next base or installation. Before you know it, you will also have a 20-year career and retirement! I've helped thousands of military spouses change their lives and I hope this book will help thousands more.

THIS BOOK IS DEDICATED TO INSPIRE YOU to pursue a federal career, for your family stability, personal goals, quality of life, financial security and future planning (after your spouse retires or separates from the service). You deserve a fulfilling career and the opportunity to save for retirement, receive professional training, have excellent benefits and leave, and get promoted.

Good luck, and write to me if you get hired into the government as a military spouse. I love success stories!

Kathryn Troutman, former U.S. Navy Military Spouse, Author and Publisher
kathryn@resume-place.com

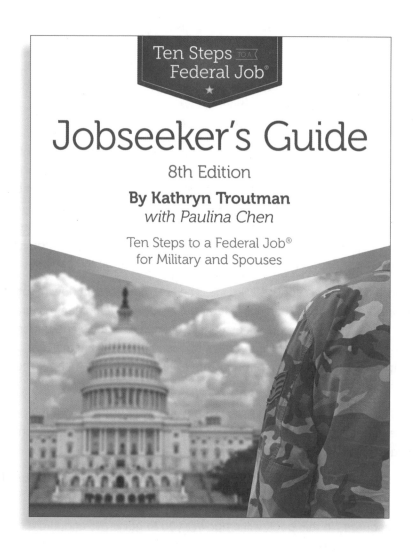

The Stars Are Lined Up for Military Spouses is the companion guide to the *Jobseeker's Guide 8th Edition*.

Refer to the *Jobseeker's Guide* for more in-depth information about the Ten Steps to a Federal Job.

http://www.fedjobtraining.com/books/jobseekers-guide

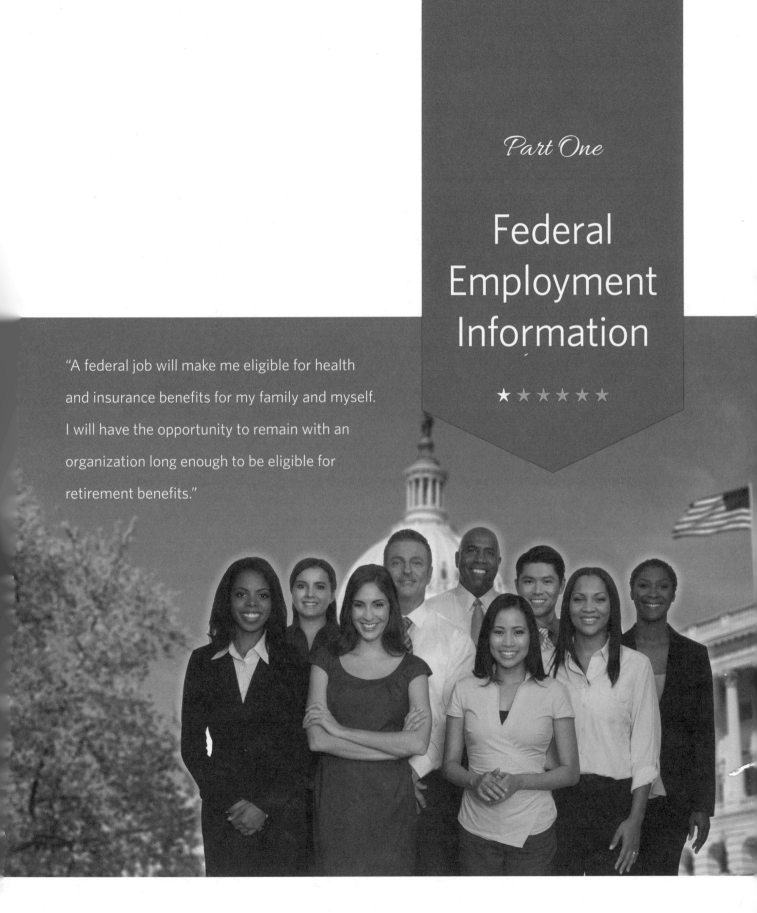

Part One

Federal Employment Information

★ ★ ★ ★ ★ ★

"A federal job will make me eligible for health and insurance benefits for my family and myself. I will have the opportunity to remain with an organization long enough to be eligible for retirement benefits."

Federal Employment Information

Applying for a federal job is challenging and competitive, but the good news for military spouses is that the federal government has provided a few benefits that can help give you a boost when applying for a federal job. The goal of this book is to help you learn about these benefits and how to use them in your federal job search.

Furthermore, those of you who are overseas can also take advantage of different types of federal jobs, such as Nonappropriated Fund (NAF) jobs and Excepted Service positions that are located at your base.

Federal job and job search benefits suitable for military spouses

Program S (Priority Placement Program)	Eligible military spouses may apply for federal jobs at Department of Defense (DOD) agencies with benefits for application placement and priority.
Merit and Competitive Positions	Military spouses may apply for positions open to "Federal Employees" and positions open to "U.S. Citizens" (if they are U.S. citizens).
Excepted Service	Some positions or agencies fall under Excepted Service, which are sometimes temporary positions ranging from one to four years and provide the same benefits and promotion opportunities as Merit and Competitive federal positions.
Nonappropriated Funds (NAF)	NAF jobs are available on all military bases with the same benefits as General Schedule (GS) federal jobs. Many positions are with the Morale, Welfare, and Recreation activities.
Derived Preference	Family members may utilize a military member's 10 point preference for special consideration.

USAJOBS.gov

Federal jobs are mostly posted on USAJOBS.gov. It is easy to find federal positions at your next base using USAJOBS.gov. Just type in the base or installation or city and state, and you will find the positions. The search below is for Fort Bragg, NC. There are 331 jobs right now. There are 239 positions that are open to the public and 106 federal employee positions.

Federal Career Benefits

Starting Benefits for New Federal Employees

★ 26 days leave (combination of annual and sick leave/year for a full-time federal employee with 0-3 years of service)

★ 10 paid holidays

★ Some telework (negotiated) and alternative work schedules

★ Family-friendly employer and sometimes daycare facilities

★ Career advancement based on performance, skills, and opportunity

★ Greater job stability than in private industry

Grade levels that military spouses are being appointed to:

Employment by New Grade/Salary Group

		Federal Civilian Workfoce	Veterans	Disabled Veterans	Derived Preference	Military Spouse Appointment*
SES		0.39%	0.22%	0.09%	0.09%	0.00%
GS, GM, GL	Grade 1-4	3.41%	2.17%	2.73%	5.58%	27.47%
	Grade 5-8	17.86%	19.02%	22.26%	32.80%	51.08%
	Grade 9-12	30.51%	32.45%	36.49%	30.50%	15.70%
	Grade 13-15	19.53%	16.06%	14.61%	12.85%	1.12%
Blue Collar Pay Plans		8.53%	15.10%	13.18%	7.12%	3.82%
Other White Collar Pay Plans		19.78%	14.99%	10.64%	11.05%	0.80%

This table is revised since General Schedule and Related(GSR)Pay Plans are no longer generated.

*Noncompetitive Appointment of Certain Military Spouses Hiring Authority was effective September 11, 2009 authorized by Executive Order 13473.

Federal Salaries

Based on military spouse and GS grade level studies, 15% of military spouses are GS-9 (see chart on previous page). The GS levels you can qualify for will depend on your years of work experience, specialized experience, and education. Each USAJOBS announcement will state clearly the QUALIFICATIONS REQUIRED.

If you are trying to qualify for a GS level based on education alone, you are automatically qualified with these levels of education:

★ GS-4 – Two years above high school (or AA Degree)

★ GS-5 – Based on Bachelor's Degree

★ GS-7 – One full year of graduate study

★ GS-9 – Master's degree or equivalent

★ GS-11 – Ph.D.

Good news! Many federal positions do NOT require a degree beyond a high school diploma. All of the positions in the 0301 Administrative / Analyst job series do NOT require a bachelor's degree.

Salary Levels

The GS base salary for GS-9 step 1 is $43,251, and step 10 is $56,229. The base salary does not include locality pay for regions with a high cost of living, such as southern CA, Hawaii, Washington DC, or New York City. If you start in this position at a GS-9, in one year, you could be promoted to or apply for a GS-11, which has a salary range of $52,329 to $68,025. View the GS salary schedule on page 14.

Promotion Potential

If you land a GS-9 position with a promotion potential to GS-12, that means that you may be promoted all the way to a GS-12 without applying for a new position. Keep an eye out for these "career ladder" vacancy announcements!

Negotiating Your Salary and Benefits

If you receive a federal job offer, sometimes you can negotiate your federal job benefits, including a higher step, if you have specialized experience, training, or other qualifications. To negotiate a higher step, you would write a Superior Qualifications Letter to provide justification for your request. See a sample Superior Qualifications Letter in the *Jobseeker's Guide 8th edition* (Step 10).

Work-Life Benefits

Available Leave Options and Work Schedule Flexibilities

The federal government offers a wide range of leave options and workplace flexibilities to assist an employee who needs to be away from the workplace. These include annual leave, sick leave, advanced annual leave or advanced sick leave, leave under the Family and Medical Leave Act (FMLA), donated leave under voluntary leave bank programs, leave without pay, alternative work schedules, credit hours under flexible work schedules, compensatory time off, and telework. Each agency also has an Employee Assistance Program (EAP)—a voluntary, confidential program that helps employees work through various life challenges.

Alternative Work Schedules

Alternative work schedules allow employees to complete their 80 hours of work with scheduling flexibility over a 10-day, bi-weekly period. There are two categories of alternative work schedules—compressed workweek programs and flexible workday schedules.

Telework

Under an agency's telework policy, an employee may be permitted to work at home or at another worksite. Telework may also be used in conjunction with paid leave or other workplace flexibilities and can provide employees with valuable additional time for dependent care responsibilities by reducing commuting time or by allowing employees to temporarily care for a family member who resides in a different geographic location. For more information, go to https://www.telework.gov.

Childcare

Many federal agencies provide assistance to employees facing childcare challenges, such as on-site childcare, resource and referral services, and the childcare subsidy program. Federal employees also have access to Dependent Care Flexible Spending Accounts (FSAs), which can be used for child care, before- and after-school care, nursery and preschool, and summer day camp.

Pregnancy/Childbirth

A pregnant employee who must be absent from work at some point before giving birth for her own health or that of her unborn child is entitled to use sick leave. An employee is also entitled to use sick leave to care for a family member who is incapacitated because of pregnancy or childbirth, or to accompany her to prenatal care appointments. New parents are entitled to use leave under FMLA for the birth of a child and care of the newborn.

Elder Care

The Dependent Care FSA may also be used to care for a relative who lives in your home and is incapable of self-care.

Retirement and Insurance

Retirement/Pension

The Federal Employees Retirement System (FERS) is a three-tiered plan to provide secure retirement, disability, and survivor benefits for employees and their dependents. In addition to Social Security benefits as a base, FERS offers both an annuity that grows with length of service and a tax deferred savings plan. Employees are fully vested after five years of service and, for disability benefits, after just 18 months. For more information on FERS, see https://www.opm.gov/retirement-services/fers-information/.

Life Insurance

Term life insurance is available to federal employees at group rates. Most full-time and part-time employees are automatically enrolled in Basic Life Insurance equal to their salary, rounded to the next $1,000, plus $2,000. The government pays one-third of the cost of this group term insurance. There are also three types of "Optional" life insurance under which the employee pays the full cost.

Health Insurance

Federal employees can enroll in health insurance coverage for themselves and their families at reasonable group rates. They enjoy one of the widest selections of plans in the country. Over 200 plans participate in the health insurance program. Employees can choose among: fee-for-service plans, health maintenance organization plans, consumer-driven health plans, and high deductible health plans. Federal employees share the cost with the government with most full-time employees paying 25% of the total premium. Federal employees may also be eligible for dental and vision insurance at unsubsidized group rates.

Flexible Spending Accounts

Federal employees have the opportunity to set aside pre-tax money to fund federal Flexible Spending Accounts (FSAs). There are two different types of accounts available: Health Care Flexible Spending Accounts and Dependent Care Flexible Spending Accounts.

Federal Long-Term Care Insurance

Federal employees are eligible to apply for federal long-term care to defray the costs of such care. There are a number of plan choices and features that can be customized to meet employee needs and the needs of eligible family members.

GS Salary Table

2017 GS Salary Rates by Grade and Step

The General Schedule (GS) is a worldwide pay system that covers more than 1.5 million employees. The GS pay scale has 15 grades and 10 steps in each grade.

Pay varies by geographic location. Be sure to look up your potential salary WITH your locality pay!

★ Washington, DC / Baltimore: add 27.10% to the base salary

★ San Diego, CA: add 26.98% to the base salary

★ Kauai, Hawaii: add 17.92% to the base salary and 11.32% for COLA

Grade	Step 1	Step 2	Step 3	Step 4	Step 5	Step 6	Step 7	Step 8	Step 9	Step 10	Within Grade
1	18526	19146	19762	20375	20991	21351	21960	22575	22599	23171	VARIES
2	20829	21325	22015	22599	22853	23525	24197	24869	25541	26213	VARIES
3	22727	23485	24243	25001	25759	26517	27275	28033	28791	29549	758
4	25514	26364	27214	28064	28914	29764	30614	31464	32314	33164	850
5	28545	29497	30449	31401	32353	33305	34257	35209	36161	37113	952
6	31819	32880	33941	35002	36063	37124	38185	39246	40307	41368	1061
7	35359	36538	37717	38896	40075	41254	42433	43612	44791	45970	1179
8	39159	40464	41769	43074	44379	45684	46989	48294	49599	50904	1305
9	43251	44693	46135	47577	49019	50461	51903	53345	54787	56229	1442
10	47630	49218	50806	52394	53982	55570	57158	58746	60334	61922	1588
11	52329	54073	55817	57561	59305	61049	62793	64537	66281	68025	1744
12	62722	64813	66904	68995	71086	73177	75268	77359	79450	81541	2091
13	74584	77070	79556	82042	84528	87014	89500	91986	94472	96958	2486
14	88136	91074	94012	96950	99888	102826	105764	108702	111640	114578	2938
15	103672	107128	110584	114040	117496	120952	124408	127864	131320	134776	3456

Source: www.opm.gov/policy-data-oversight/pay-leave/salaries-wages/2017/general-schedule/

Part One

Classification Standards

Find Your Job Series and Position Descriptions

If you're wondering where to find the descriptions of federal jobs, then go to the classification standards. The classification standards list all federal positions and include the typical skills required for each. These descriptions are invaluable for writing your USAJOBS and Program S resumes! Use the descriptions in the work experience section of your federal resume.

Social Services Aid and Assistant Series, GS-0186   TS-66 October 1982

SERIES DEFINITION

This series covers nonprofessional positions in support of counseling, guidance, and related social services work in social, employment assistance, or similar programs. The persons served by the programs may be individuals or families in the community of individuals in an institution, dormitory, or other Government facility. Duties may range from work that involves group leadership and giving practical guidance on day-to-day activities to residents in a Government facility to work that involves giving unemployed adults information and assistance on community job training or employment opportunities. The work requires skill to communicate effectively and to work constructively with members of the particular group involved. The work also requires a practical knowledge of program requirements and procedures, and a practical understanding of some of the more routine methods and techniques of counseling.

What Is a Competitive Federal Resume?

From the *Federal Resume Guidebook 6th Edition* by Kathryn Troutman, pages 14–16

3 to 5 Pages in Length

The federal resume must include certain information in order for you to be rated as Best Qualified for a position. Each generalized and specialized skill that you have developed in your career has to be written into the document.

Matches the Job Announcement

To be successful, the federal resume must match the job announcement by making sure KEYWORDS are very easy to find and showing how how you have the knowledge, skills, and abilities for the job, including those listed in the Questionnaire that is Part 2 of the federal job application.

Includes Accomplishments

In order to be rated Best Qualified, you must include accomplishments demonstrating excellent past performance.

Lists Employment in Reverse Chronological Order

This order is used by the Resume Builder in USAJOBS.gov. Refer to the USAJOBS Resume Builder to make sure your federal resume includes the required information.

Includes Information Required in Your Federal Resume

The federal resume must match the USAJOBS Resume Builder fields. We recomend that you use the USAJOBS Resume Builder to create your resume for the first time.

- ★ Month and year of each job you held for at least the last 10 years
- ★ Supervisor names and phone numbers (if they are available)
- ★ Street addresses, city, state, and zip code of employers for at least 10 years
- ★ Education with hours completed
- ★ Majors and colleges with city, state, and zip code
- ★ Training with titles, sponsoring organizations, and classroom hours

And last but not least...

Uses the Outline Format!

The Best Federal Resume Format

USAJOBS resumes are read by human resources specialists, not by an automated system.

The **Outline Format** was developed by Kathryn Troutman in the first edition of the *Federal Resume Guidebook* in 1996 and is the preferred format by human resources specialists for readability!

Coastal Development Services
3704 Pacific Avenue, Suite 100
Virginia Beach, VA   23451 United States

11/2015 – Present
Salary: 45,000 USD Per Year
Hours per week: 40
General Clerk III

Paragraphs, not bullets

Duties, Accomplishments and Related Skills:
PAY ADMINISTRATION: Maintain officer and enlisted military pay accounts for 3,708 personnel assigned to supported commands and activities per pertinent directives. Provide information and advice to military customers on all pay, electronic service record entries, dependency data guidelines/updates, and benefits/entitlements.

INVESTIGATIONS AND PROBLEM-SOLVING: Investigate issues and maintain knowledge on the current Military Personnel Manual, Command Pass Coordinator Manual and all other Department of Defense instructions. Analyze military records for discrepancies and deficiencies.

ALL CAPS headlines for each paragraph using KEYWORDS from the announcement

EDUCATION SERVICES, CONSULTATION, AND TRAINING: Provide on one consulting and training. Effectively counseled 290 person   n and training opportunities. Properly ordered and prepared adva   heets and administered Navy-wide advancement examinations wit   discrepancies. Approved 57 tuition assistance requests for pe   g higher education.

DATA, RECORDS, AND SYSTEMS MANAGEMENT: Provide clerical support and data entry. Operate automated systems to maintain and update electronic records. Prepare transactions by utilizing current pay/personnel input systems to repo   pay actions as outlined in Department of Defense guidelines and directives Provide pay and personnel services to Navy personnel utilizing TOPS, NSI   nd MMPA systems with the uppermost attention to detail. Perform compu   entry and information processing. Maintain records in a filing system t   records in an orderly manner.

Add your accomplishments at the end of each job block

KEY ACCOMPLISHMENTS: Successfully determined the legal and appropriate eligibility of pay entitlements. Commended for ability to operate computerized programs and databases in order to enter, modify, and retrieve sensitive information into and from electronic service records and or reports in a timely and accurate manner. Recognized for effectively processing all required documents for seven (7) personnel advancing through the Command Advancement Program.

What to Include in Your Federal Resume

Personal Information

★ Full name, mailing address (with zip code), day and evening phone numbers (with area codes), and email address (one that you can access outside work if necessary)

Work Experience

Give the following information for your paid and unpaid work experience related to the job you are applying for (do not send job descriptions):

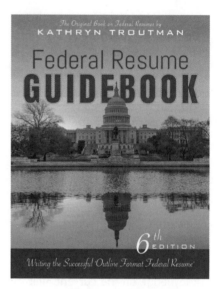

★ Job title (include series and grade if it was a federal job)

★ Duties and accomplishments

★ Employer's name and address, city, state, and zip code

★ Supervisor's name and phone number (if you have this)

★ Starting and ending dates (month and year)

★ Hours per week

★ Salary (optional, not required)

★ Indicate whether you give permission to contact your current supervisor (saying "no" is acceptable and will not affect your chances of being considered for the position)

Write your best federal resume with the *Federal Resume Guidebook 6th Edition* by Kathryn Troutman

Education

★ Colleges or universities

★ Name, city, and state (zip code)

★ Majors

★ Type and year of any degrees received (if no degree, show total credits earned and indicate whether semester or quarter hours)

★ Copy of your college transcript (if requested), upload in USAJOBS account

Other Qualifications

★ Job-related training courses (title and year/classroom hours and certificate if you received this)

★ Job-related skills, e.g., other languages, computer software/hardware, and typing speed

★ Job-related certificates and licenses (current only)

★ Job-related honors, awards, and special accomplishments; for example, publications, memberships in professional or honor societies, leadership activities, public speaking, and performance awards (give dates but do not send documents unless requested)

This information is listed in the OPM OF-510, Applying for a Federal Job
www.gpo.gov/pdfs/careers/apply/of0510.pdf

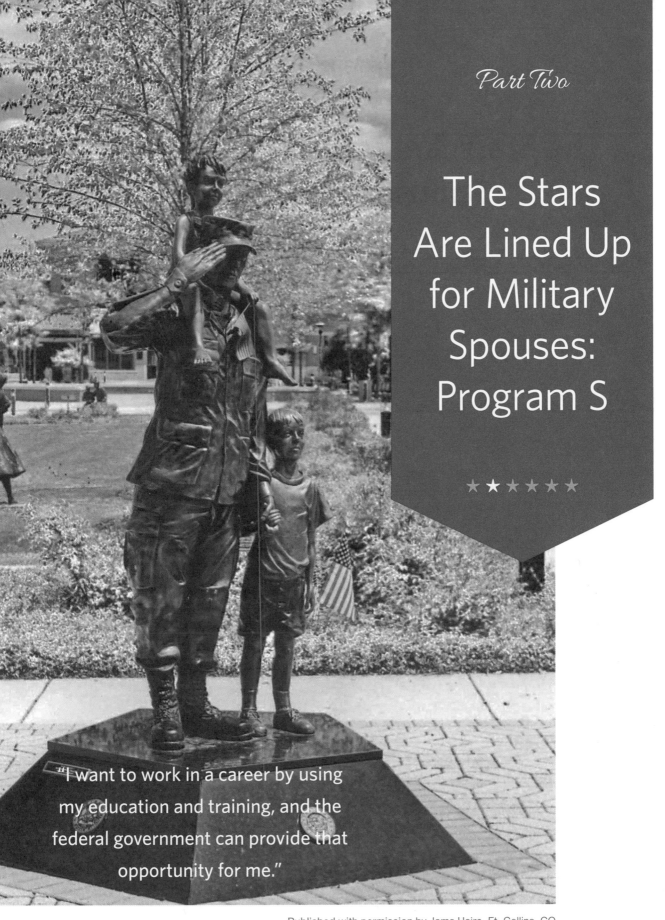

Part Two

The Stars Are Lined Up for Military Spouses: Program S

★ ★ ★ ★ ★

"I want to work in a career by using my education and training, and the federal government can provide that opportunity for me."

Published with permission by Jams Haire, Ft. Collins, CO

The Stars Are Lined Up for Military Spouses: Program S

The Department of Defense (DOD) Priority Placement Program (PPP) is a DOD-wide program that provides referrals and priority when applying for Department of Defense civilian jobs. Military spouses may also participate in the PPP under Program S, also known as PPP-S.

How It Works

1 Register for the PPP, which is a separate database from USAJOBS.

2 HR will let you know you are matched to a position on USAJOBS. Or you can search for matching jobs yourself.

3 Apply in USAJOBS.

4 If Best Qualified, you may receive priority during the application process.

Follow the STARS in Program S

- ★ Star 1: Who Qualifies for Program S?
- ★ Star 2: Write Your Federal Resume
- ★ Star 3: Find Your Documents
- ★ Star 4: Set Up Your Program S Meeting
- ★ Star 5: Improve Your Program S Registry

- ★ Star 6: PPP Match Notification
- ★ Star 7: Apply for Jobs on USAJOBS
- ★ Star 8: Save a Search for Job Matches
- ★ Star 9: Follow Up on USAJOBS
- ★ Star 10: Get Best Qualified

Eligibility: Does Not Expire

GOOD NEWS MILITARY SPOUSES!
BIG CHANGE - EO 13473 - NDAA 2017
Elimination of two-year eligibility limitation
for noncompetitive appointment of spouses
of members of the armed forces.

Program S eligibility no longer expires after two years!

POLICY: Impact of the FY2017 National Defense Authorization Act (NDAA) on Program S Registrants

DATE ISSUED: 31 January 2017

Pursuant to Section 1131 of the FY 2017 National Defense Authorization Act (NDAA), which was enacted on December 23, 2016, **the two-year eligibility limitation for noncompetitive appointment of spouses of members of the Armed Forces was eliminated**. This change removed the time limitation for the noncompetitive appointment of military spouses subsequent to each Permanent Change of Station (PCS) move they make with their military sponsors without altering the limitation to one permanent appointment per qualifying PCS as previously authorized by Executive Order (E.O.) 13473 and codified in 5 CFR 315.612. Therefore, military spouses may be appointed on the basis of the authority without further regard to the two-year limitation on the appointment eligibility.

In light of this change, military spouses registered in Program S of the Priority Placement Program (PPP) on the basis of the E.O. 13473 appointment eligibility and who reached their two-year eligibility limitation on December 23, 2016 or later may remain registered in the PPP as long as they are otherwise eligible (i.e., married to the sponsor, within the commuting area of the sponsor's permanent duty station, have not received a continuing offer of federal employment, etc.). As such, registering activities must review Program S registrations that expired on or after December 23, 2016 to ensure that affected spouses are afforded continued registration. Further, until such time as Chapter 14 of the PPP Handbook is updated, registering activities are advised to redact references to the two-year expiration of E.O. 13473 appointability on the Program S Registration Counseling Checklist when accomplishing new Program S registrations.

Star 1

Who Qualifies for Program S?

The first thing to understand is that the PPP registry is open to more than just military spouses.

Eligibility for PPP registry

★ Current or former career or career-conditional federal employee

★ Executive Order (E.O.) 13473 eligible (military spouses)

★ E.O. 12721 eligible (expires after three years)

★ Reinstatement eligible

★ Current Veterans Recruitment Authority (VRA) or Schedule A appointee for persons with disabilities

★ Interchange agreement eligible

Program S

Program S allows military spouses to register for PPP.

To qualify for Program S, you must meet ALL of these conditions:

★ Spouse of active duty military member of the U.S. Armed Forces, (including U.S. Coast Guard and full-time National Guard and Reserve)

★ Sponsor (spouse) is assigned by a Permanent Change of Station (PCS) Order

★ Spouse accompanies sponsor to new and permanent duty station (PDS)

★ Must be married prior to your sponsor's REPORTING DATE to the new PDS

★ Must meet all pre-employment criteria

★ Must be eligible for immediate non-competitive appointment to a position in the Competitive Service

Termination of Eligibility

You will no longer be eligible for Program S if any of the following occur:

★ You accept or decline a continuing DOD (permanent) appropriated or NAF position within commuting distance of the PDS (this applies to federal positions you may apply to on your own [without preference], not just Program S positions)

★ You accept a DOD position outside the commuting area of the sponsor's PDS

★ You no longer meet eligibility requirements (e.g., loss of spousal status or refusal to participate in the established process)

★ You have less than six months remaining at the duty station

★ At least 12 months have gone by since your initial registration or last extension

★ ★ ★ ★ ★

Part Two

E.O. 13473 Requirements

DEPARTMENT OF DEFENSE

DCPAS

Defense Civilian Personnel Advisory Service

MILITARY SPOUSE PREFERENCE PROGRAM (PROGRAM S)
Priority Placement Program Fact Sheet

Military Spouse Appointing Authority (Executive Order [E.O.] 13473) allows agencies to appoint a military spouse without competition. Agencies can choose to use this authority when filling competitive service positions on a temporary (not to exceed one year), term (more than one year but not more than four years), or permanent basis. The authority does not entitle spouses to an appointment over any other applicant.

As a military spouse you are eligible under this authority if your active duty military spouse: 1) receives a Permanent Change of Station (PCS) move; 2) has a 100% disability rating; or 3) died while on active duty. Each of these categories has different eligibility criteria that must be met.

Active Duty Spouse PCS: As a military spouse you must:

★ Be authorized to relocate on the PCS orders

★ Actually relocate to the new duty station

Military spouses can only be appointed within the reasonable daily commuting distance of the new duty station and the appointment. The military spouse can use the PCS orders for an unlimited time at each PCS installation. You will be asked to provide a copy of the PCS orders.

Based on 100% Disability: You are eligible if your active duty spouse:

★ Retired under Chapter 61 of Title 10, United States Code with a 100% disability rating from the military department

★ Retired or was released from active duty and has a disability rating of 100% from the Department of Veterans Affairs or the military department

There is no geographic limitation under this category. You will be required to provide documentation of your spouse's disability.

Based on Service Member's Death: If your spouse was killed while on active duty and you are not remarried, you are eligible. There is no geographic limitation in this category. You will be required to provide documentation of the death and your marital status at the time of death.

Note: Military Spouse Preference is a Department of Defense program applicable to positions being filled both in the continental United States and at overseas locations. For more information contact your local Department of Defense personnel office.

Which Federal Jobs Qualify?

yes

★ DOD positions

★ Competitive Service (not Excepted Service) jobs

★ Within commuting distance of new location

★ U.S. and its territories or possessions

no

★ Non-DOD jobs

★ Positions filled through non-competitive procedures

★ Positions in the Excepted Service

★ Positions in foreign areas

★ NAF positions

★ Delegated Examining Unit or Direct Hire Authority announcements

★ Component career programs

★ Positions in the Defense Civilian Intelligence Personnel System and those in organizations that have intelligence, counter-intelligence, or national security as a primary function

Sample PCS Orders

UNITED STATES MARINE CORPS
U. S. MARINE CORPS FORCES CYBERSPACE COMMAND
9800 SAVAGE ROAD
FORT GEORGE G MEADE, MARYLAND 20755

IN REPLY REFER TO:
1320
CPAC
9 Jun 16

FIRST ENDORSEMENT on CMC Washington DC Web Orders of 14 March 2016

From: Director, Consolidated Personnel Administrative Center
To:

Subj: PERMANENT CHANGE OF STATION ORDERS

1. Delivered. Effective 0800, 1 July 2016 you will stand detached from your present station and duties and report by 2359, 13 July 2016 to COMMANDING OFFICER, 1ST INTEL BN MHG I MEF, BOX 555321, CAMP PENDLETON, CALIFORNIA 92055 (MCC 114) for duty.

2. You are authorized 0 day(s) proceed, 0 day(s) PDMRA, 4 day(s) delay chargeable as annual leave, and 8 day(s) travel via Mixed Modes in reporting to your new duty station. Your projected leave balance upon completion of authorized delay is 113 day(s) accrued. Your dependents authorized travel under these orders are:

Dependent Name	Relationship	DOB/Gain

3. Should an emergency arise and you determine that more leave is required, contact your new command. Your request must include the reason, number of days requested, leave address, telephone number and your leave balance. You have given your leave address as: -----. You have given the person to be notified in case of emergency as: -----. Any change of leave address shall be reported to the Commanding Officer of your new duty station.

4. Before making any rental or lease agreements or purchasing a home, you will report to the local military family housing office at your new duty station. You will submit your travel claim to the disbursing officer at your new duty station within 5 days after completion of travel to settle travel expenses. Failure to comply will result in your pay account being checked for your travel advance. Additionally, elapsed time will be charged as leave if your travel claim has not been submitted to the disbursing officer within 30 days after completion of travel under these orders.

5. Your estimated travel entitlement is $---- based on data at the time the order was issued. This amount is 80% of your total estimated PCS allowances. It does not include any adjustments based on your outbound interview answers. If traveling on Government procured transportation your reimbursement amount will be lower than this estimate. The actual amount of final entitlements will be computed upon settlement of your travel claim.

Star
2

Write Your Federal Resume

Match Your Resume to the
PPP Handbook Chapter 10 Option Codes

A human resources specialist will be reviewing your resume and scoring it in terms of the potential grade level, occupational series, and Program S option codes (knowledge, skills and abilities) that your resume represents. Your resume is critical to the success of your Program S registration score and the possible matches to USAJOBS positions.

What are the Program S Option Codes?

Find the Option Code list in the appendix of this book.

You can qualify for up to 10 Option Codes per job series.

The more Option Codes you qualify for, the more matches you could receive!

CHAPTER 10

OPTION CODES

A. PURPOSE

The purpose of this Chapter is to explain the proper use of option codes, which are used in registration to more specifically define qualifications and in requisitioning to clarify job requirements.

B. PROCEDURAL REQUIREMENTS

Except for the six generic options (see B.6., below) and the NOA option code (see B.2. below), option codes may be used only with the specific occupational series under which they are listed in Appendix A.

1. The registration format will accommodate up to 10 option codes per skill line. Decisions as to which options, if any, may be used, are based solely on a registrant's qualifications. An option code should never be entered more than once for the same occupational series.

Case Study: Bobbi Robbins

Bobbi Robbins moved from Okinawa to Ft. Meade, MD on PCS with her U.S. Navy military spouse. Bobbi came to work at The Resume Place, Inc. as a Ten Steps to a Federal Job Coordinator. Around the same time, The Resume Place began working on the curriculum and book, *The Stars Are Lined Up for Military Spouses*. So, Bobbi became the first case study for the Program S cases and the STARS method in this book! This page shows Bobbi's first Program S registration. She was scored for her grade level GS-7 or 9, and they scored her for four occupational series: 0101, 0186, 0301 and 0303. Kathryn Troutman, author of the book, accompanied Bobbi to her interview with the HRO at Ft. Meade, MD. Kathryn and Bobbi were both disappointed with the Option Codes for the four series. She got only three Option Codes: EAP, NOA, and FSP. Bobbi added more content to her resume and sent it back to HRO for a new score. Bobbi moved from Ft. Meade before she could land a position with Program S in the local area. But she continues to pursue her Program S position now at Camp Pendleton, CA.

-- EXPERIENCE --		FROM		TO
		201402		201504
		200911		201302
-- SKILLS --	PG	SER	HI	LO
	GS	0101	09	09
	Options: EAP FSP			
	GS	0186	07	07
	Options: NOA			
	GS	0301	09	09
	Options: FSP NOA			
	GS	0303	07	07
	Options: FSP			

Bobbi's Option Codes from the first Program S meeting

Option Code descriptions

101	Social Service		ADC	Alcohol & Drug Control Officer
			EAP	Employee Assistance Program Coordinator
			EFM	Exceptional Family Member Program
			FAP	Family Advocacy Program
			FSP	Family Support Services

301 & 303	(con't)		FSP	Family Support Services
			FUL	Fuels/Energy
			HCA	Health Care
			HOA	Housing
			INS	Information Systems Management
			ITN	International Affairs

Bobbi Robbins' Program S Resume

BOBBI ROBBINS

1020 Edmondson Ave. • Baltimore, MD 21228
555-555-5555 • bobbir@gmail.com
Military Spouse • U.S. Citizen

SPOUSE PREFERENCE: Spouse of Active Duty USMC. Eligible for consideration under Executive Order 13473, September 11, 2009 Non-competitive Appointment for Certain Military Spouses, and DoD Priority Placement Program.

SUMMARY OF SKILLS:

Six years' experience in employment readiness counseling, case management, employment training coordination, and database maintenance. Specialized knowledge in federal employment, military spouse and veterans preference for federal careers. Effective webinar instructor and training coordinator. Effective in customer services, attention to detail and follow-up. Proficient in information databases: Adobe Quickbase, Excel, Google Doc management; gotomeeting.com systems; Constant Contact updates; mail-merge, survey development and study tracking systems.

PROFESSIONAL EXPERIENCE

Series: 0301, 0303
Admin
No Option Codes

EMPLOYMENT SERVICES AND TRAINING COORDINATOR
Federal Career Training Institute and
The Resume Place, Inc., Catonsville, MD

02/2014 – Present
40 Hours per Week

FEDERAL EMPLOYMENT READINESS CONSULTANT: Review client resumes and federal job targets to determine congruence among their eligibility, career goals, and the target job field. Counsel students, private industry, current federal employees, military veterans, and spouse clients on their career objectives and direct them towards federal job resources.

CLIENT ASSIGNMENT: Oversee federal resume case management, encompassing a range of clientele seeking consulting, training, and writing services for federal employment. Review client objectives and clarify the scope of work purchased. Evaluate workloads, schedules, and writer specialties to assign projects to 20+ professional staff.

TRAINING COORDINATOR, TEN STEPS TO A FEDERAL JOB™: Coordinate registrations; provide training support, materials delivery for military and university career and employment counselors worldwide.   Follow-up after live and webinar trainings to manage evaluations, materials and ten steps material distribution. Produce invoices and discuss Ten Step training program materials and resources with purchase officers.

WEBINAR INSTRUCTOR: Using gotomeeting.com technology, teach 30-minute webinars to federal applicants, including Ten Steps to a Federal Job™. Coordinate and act as facilitator for webinar series with other panelists. Set up webinar classes online and provide PowerPoints and handouts for webinar classes. Manage course evaluations.

MAINTAIN THE CLIENT AND TRAINING DATABASES: Using Adobe Quickbase and Excel in Google docs maintain annual certifications and ensure that registrations and licenses are maintained. For resume service clients, maintain the same database for client information, documents, project estimates and assignments. Follow-through to ensure data is up-to-date.

PROJECT MANAGEMENT: Serve as the Team Leader for a major project aimed at leveraging resources and technology to improve client tracking and success rates. Conduct data analysis across multiple databases and collaborate with staff to revise reporting procedures. Develop customer satisfaction surveys and coordinate ongoing work standardization efforts.

CUSTOMER SERVICE: Deliver high-quality support and service to all customers through effective communication, tactfulness, and a professional demeanor. Provide project cost estimates and interact with clients via phone, email, and other written correspondence. Manage and resolve client complaints, and coordinate with staff members and subcontractors to ensure client satisfaction.

Key Accomplishments:

- Improved communication with past Ten Steps Certified trainers through updated correspondence to support our three year Ten Steps License.
- Supported the creation of a database that tracked the Ten Step classes being taught worldwide by licensed trainers and the number of classes taught per base. Recognized that more than 226 military bases were licensed to teach Ten Steps to a Federal Job in 2012; and more than 12,000 of the Ten Steps text – Jobseeker Guide were supporting the Ten Steps curriculum. Created new data to recognize the importance of federal employment training for military spouses, transitioning military and civilians.
- Improved the resume client database system to improve tracking, customer services data and client results information. Designed a survey and received results from 140 federal resume clients.

Series: 0101 Social Science, 0303 Clerk & Assist
Option Codes: EAP/FSP

FAMILY READINESS OFFICER (NF-0301-04)   11/2009 – 02/2013
Marine Corps Community Services, Camp Schwab, Okinawa, Japan   40 Hours per Week

CLIENT SUPPORT & NEEDS ASSESSMENTS: Conducted biannual surveys to assess needs of families and personnel to increase the program's value. Assisted clients in prioritizing issues/developing plans and goals tailored to meet specific needs. Provided support and assistance to the Marines, Sailors, and their families through weekly informational email communications and newsletters.

WORK & FAMILY LIFE EXPERT: Managed the presence of program resource specialists at major unit events to increase accessibility. Fostered support systems for new and less experienced FROs through mentorship. Connected outbound personnel and family members with FROs at their gaining command.

VOLUNTEER RECRUITMENT AND COORDINATION: Interviewed and supervised a team of 11 Family Readiness Assistants and Command Team Advisors. Coordinated annual volunteer recognition events.

COMMUNICATION MANAGEMENT: Used MS Excel, MS Outlook, and Marine Online to maintain distribution lists of up to 750 Marines spread throughout six companies and their family members. Used distribution lists to facilitate home and section visits as well as telephone, post, and email communications to maximize awareness of the program and to connect eligible persons with needed support services.

CONDUCTED INTERVIEWS: Conducted interviews to establish the nature and extent of concerns and issues posed by military family members. Provided assistance in developing personal and family-based goals and plans. Collaborated with social service delivery systems in the military and civilian community to manage clients and ensure positive results.

FINANCIAL MANAGEMENT & ADVICE: Managed annual Unit Family Readiness budgets of up to $17,000. Allocated funds and donated items while ensuring that spending stayed within the guidelines stipulated for Non-Appropriated Funds. Provided the Commander with weekly informational updates on the program's financial status.

NEWSLETTER WRITING & EDITING: Utilized various software-based systems, such as SharePoint and resource websites, to gather information for inclusion in the weekly email. Used MS Word to develop and publish a weekly newsletter. Built and maintained the unit's e-Marine website to serve as an additional reference point.

Series: 0101 Social Science,
0303 Clerk & Assist
Option Codes: EAP/FSP

Key Accomplishments:

- As a Family Readiness Officer at Camp Schwab, Okinawa, Japan, it was my responsibility to coordinate efforts to celebrate the unit's children. Being overseas provided challenges to facilitating such celebrations, as resources were limited and expensive to obtain off-installation. During this time, tensions with the Okinawan populace were very high due to the planned relocation of a Marine Corps Air Station. Recognizing this tension, I suggested that the children of the local children's home and orphanage should be invited onto the base for fun activities with our unit's families. I contacted the camp's Community Liaison and Public Relations Specialist and worked through him to communicate our unit's intent with the leadership at the Nagomi Children's Home in Henoko. I also coordinated with the American Red Cross to collect items that would be useful to the children in the home, as well as blankets and toys. As a result of my efforts, seventeen children and five caregivers from the children's home participated in the event along with 28 American service and family members. This was the first unit-initiated event of its kind and the first real cultural exchange opportunity for many of the families in attendance.

- Coordinated with FROs across the 3d Marine Division and other outside organizations, such as the Camp Courtney Junior Marines, to plan and execute the first-ever annual 3d Marine Division Marine Corps Birthday Ball for Kids.

VOLUNTEER EXPERIENCE

FAMILY READINESS ASSISTANT (VOLUNTEER)   07/2009 – 06/2013
Marine Corps Community Services, Okinawa, Japan   10 Hours per Week

FAMILY READINESS EXPERT: Directly supported and assisted the Family Readiness Officer (FRO) in managing the Unit Family Readiness Program. Applied in-depth knowledge of the Commander's family readiness goals and proactively coordinated with military members and their families to increase morale and quality of life. Advised on military organization, lifestyle issues, and stresses accompanying military life to enhance relationships.

Key Accomplishment:

- Successfully responded to a need for improved communication with Marines and their family members by revamping the design and content of both weekly and monthly newsletters. My efforts directly resulted in a redesigned communication campaign that was buoyed by a visually enhanced publication and a more welcoming tone.

L.I.N.K.S. MENTOR (VOLUNTEER)   02/2012 – 06/2013
Marine Corps Community Services, Okinawa, Japan   10 Hours per Week

INDIVIDUAL & TEAM MENTORING: Worked on a one-on-one and team basis to mentor service members and their families on the benefits, resources, and services available. Provided mentorship and guidance across Lifestyle, Insights, Networking, Knowledge, and Skills (LINKS).

CLASS INSTRUCTION: Instructed classes and workshops on a range of topics encompassing the military lifestyle. Delivered information at awareness/briefing sessions and presented key points to specifically targeted audiences, such as parents, children, spouses, etc. Briefed 1-2 assigned sections of the curriculum at monthly workshops of up to 40 participants.

EDUCATION

BACHELOR OF ARTS (B.A.) – 2011
University of Maryland University College
Major: Asian Studies • GPA: 3.82

BACHELOR OF ARTS (B.A.) – 2008
State University of New York at Geneseo
Major: Psychology & Human Development • GPA: 3.34

PROFESSIONAL TRAINING

Certified Federal Job Search Trainer / Certified Federal Career Coach, Federal Career Training Institute, certified Ten Steps to a Federal Job™ Trainer, June 2013 – June 3016.
L.I.N.K.S. Mentor Training (2012) • Level I Active Military Families Facilitator (2011) • Four Lenses Facilitator (2011) • SharePoint End User (2010) • Seven Habits of Highly Effective Families (2010)

TECHNICAL SKILLS

Microsoft Office Suite (Word, Excel, PowerPoint, Access) • Statistical Package for Social Sciences (SPSS) • QuickBooks • QuickBase • SharePoint • e-Marine • Marine Online

Keywords for Option Codes

The human resources specialist needs to see certain knowledge, skills, and abilities in your resume, and those can be demonstrated by specific keywords relating to a series or Option Code. Job series keywords are listed in the **classification standards** (see page 15) or in related job announcements.

In the chart below, we have extracted sample keyword lists for common Option Codes that military spouses might be trying to qualify for. If you have the experience the government is looking for in a specific job series, use these keywords to demonstrate your qualifications.

Series	Series Title	Option Code	Option TItle	Keywords
101	Social Services	EAP	Employee Assistance Program Coordinator	Interpret regulations, policies Assess clients and determine services Develop and delivery training related to EAP Negotiate agreements to correct EAP inadequacies Knowledge of EAP programs Knowledge of EAP requirements Administrative Communications Review medical and educational forms Electronic medical records systems Complete medical and educational forms Assist customers with identifying programs/services
101	Social Services	FAP	Family Advocacy Program	Domestic abuse victim advocacy Child advocacy Working with non-offending parent Child abuse and domestic abuse Crisis intervention Safety planning and procedures Civilian and military orders of protection Dynamics of domestic, interpersonal, and family violence Knowledge of community services Laws of family relationships Prepare court testimony Crisis situations Oral communications
101	Social Services	VAR	Victim Advocate	Victim Support Services Administrative duties Victim advocacy services Victim support services Administrative duties Advocacy Services to victims or survivors of sexual assault and sexual harrassment Conduct assessments with clients Evaluate needs and risks Recognize need for professional intervention Refer to appropriate services Maintain partnerships with community Conduct training / seminars

Series	Series Title	Option Code	Option Title	Keywords
101, 301, 303	Social Services, Program Analysis, Miscellaneous Clerk and Assistant	SAR	Sexual Assault Response Coordinator	Four year degree in behavior health and social science Experience with victims of sexual assault or victim advocacy service Knowledge of DOD SAPR Knowledge of local, state, and federal laws and miltiary regulations Traiing and briefings Program development plans Sensitivity and empathy for victims Build trust with socially-diverse victims and families Analytical skills for crisis situations Work cooperatively with military and civilian legal and medical institutions Written and oral communications skills Data collection and management report production
201 & 203	Human Resources Management/Assistance	STF	Staffing	Conduct job analysis Create occupational questionnaires and vacancy announcements Determine qualifications to develop a referral list Research civilian personnel regulations Resolve staffing issues Automated staffing tools Fundamental classification and position management laws Civilian HR classification and processes
301	Miscellaneous Administration and Program	ANA	Analysis and Planning	Identify potential benefits / uses of automation Improve efficiency of administrative support Research new or improved business practices Process and audit data files for work operations Analyze and evaluate (quantitative or qualitative basis) Develop procedures to improve control systems Research new or improved business practices
301	Misc Admin and Program Management, Misc Clerk and Assistant	TRB	Training-Education	Knowledge of financial or budget transactions Knowledge of budget or financial regulations Ability to resolve complaints or discrepancies Advise on training programs / procedures Knowledge of education and training policies Processes for on-the-job, career development classes Knowledge of personnel data system Process training and education transactions Knowledge of staff functions for customer services
343	Management and Program Analyst	ACQ	Systems Acquisition	Quality of products or services Quality control, procurement, inspection, production Contracting and purchasing Supply and storage Industrial and production planning Research and engineering Maintenance Testing and evaluation Review production activities and capabilities Analyze quality data to detect unsatisfactory trends Investigate customer complaints and deficiency reports Read, interpret and apply technical data Review and evaluate supply systems operations

Series	Series Title	Option Code	Option TItle	Keywords
640	Health Aid & Technician	NUT	Nutrition	Control patient meal orders Update room service menus Provide food, nutrition and/or dietetics services Respond to calls, patient services Computerized systems for medical care Communications skills Teamwork
1102	Contract and Procurement	COL	Contract Administrator	Negotiate contract prices and terms Review contract proposals Draft contract specifications Contract administration principles Administer a group of contracts Negotiation techniques during pre-post award Price and cost analysis Monitor contractor performance to ensure compliance with contractual requirements
1702	General Education and Training	EDS	Education Services	Education theories, principles of secondary or adult education Knowledge of standardized military personnel rules Counsel on military careers Military personnel testing on careers Knowledge of career development and training concepts Knowledge of college degrees, curriculum Regulations for destruction, storage of controlled test materials Access and utilization of automated data for testing programs Counseling methods to advise on various testing programs
1702	General Education and Training	TDD	Training Design and Development	Foreign language learning Instructional methods Statistical analysis Research / evaluation Review human research protocols Develop innovations in instructional methods Learning theory, psychology of learning Instructional design practices Educational evaluation Instructional product development Human Research protection procedures Statistical analysis Improve instructional practices
2210	Information Technology Management	CSP	Customer Support	Apply systems integration methods Project management principles and methods Coordinate installation of new products or equipment Apply operating systems software principles Troubleshoot procedures Configure end user systems components Apply customer support concepts Troubleshoot and recover systems and files Coordination of installation, upgrade and maintenance Communications systems management products Third party software, security packages Scheduling systems and software packages

Star 3

Find Your Documents

Sending documents to the Human Resources Office (HRO) does not register you in Program S. That will occur after your meeting when the HRO places you in the Program S registry. Gather this information to provide it ahead of your meeting in person or via email. You will be submitting your documents for review and assessment.

Documents needed to register for Program S:

MUST HAVE:

* ★ Copy of the sponsor's PCS orders
* ★ Marriage certificate
* ★ Current federal resume

IF APPLICABLE:

* ★ Documentation of E.O. eligibility
* ★ Copy of SF-50 (for current or previous federal employees)
* ★ Most recent performance appraisal (for current or previous federal employees)
* ★ DD-214 (for military spouses who are also veterans themselves)

Add your documents to USAJOBS also!

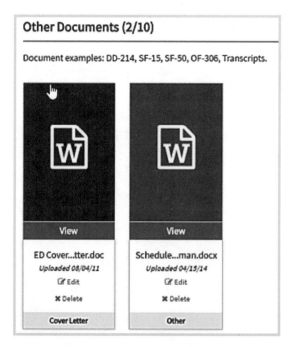

Sample Welcome Email from OCHR-San Diego, CA

Subject: Military Spouse Program

Below is the list of documents that we will need in order to verify your eligibility for the Military Spouse Priority Placement Program (PPP):

1) Original PCS ORDERS (if NAVY Service Record Page 2 Document that lists the dependents authorized to relocate)
2) Copy of most recent SF-50 or LWOP-50 (this is for current/prior federal employees only)
3) Copy of SF-75 (this is for current federal employees only)
4) DOD 10-DIGIT ID number located on the FRONT of YOUR Military Spouse ID
5) Most Recent Performance Appraisal (required for prior federal employees)
6) Copy of your Marriage Certificate
7) Electronic copy of your current narrative resume in WORD or PLAIN TEXT Format. Please watch the following video designed to help you write an effective resume at http://www.youtube.com/watch?v=XF7j03wGV6A&feature=relmfu

Also, the local Fleet and Family Support Center is also available to have their staff review your resume and provide feedback, since your resume is the most important piece of the Military Spouse PPP registration process.

The Department of the Navy (DON) posts announcements on USAJOBS (www.usajobs.gov), which is a job resource when searching for employment. In USAJOBS, an applicant can establish an account and create a saved searches file so that you will be notified by email when a vacancy opens that meets your profile. For tips on USAJOBS Advanced Searches, watch the following video at http://www.youtube.com/watch?v=c0p8mmLfdGU&feature=digest_sun

In addition to utilizing PPP for placement opportunities, military spouses are highly encouraged to apply for positions on their own. However, if a military spouse applies for a position outside of PPP, they must ensure they are eligible to apply under the "Who May Apply" section of the announcement and placement is not mandatory.

Lastly, know that there is no guarantee you will be placed through the PPP program; however, it is beneficial to begin your own job search in order to maximize your placement opportunities.

The following links provide additional information for military spouses.
http://www.fedshirevets.gov/job/shams/index.aspx
http://www.fedshirevets.gov/hire/hrp/qaspouse/index.aspx
http://www.secnav.navy.mil/donhr/How-To-Apply/Military-Spouses/Pages/Default.aspx

Regards,
HR Assistant
Department of The Navy
OCHR San Diego

Set Up Your Program S Meeting

Star 4

Make your appointment to talk to or meet your HRO representative. It might take a few phone calls or emails, but persevere in making this appointment. Your registration meeting could take up to two hours!

What to Bring: Bring a copy of your resume and other application documents.

During your appointment:

★ You will learn about Program S.

★ Expect to go through the three-page, 31-question Program S registration/counseling checklist. (See checklist in the Appendix). Initial each item after being counseled.

★ HRO will put you into the PPP-S system.

★ HRO will decide which occupational series, Option Codes, and grade levels your resume will be considered for.

★ If you previously worked for DOD, your grade level may not be higher than what you previously held. If you haven't, your grade will be determined by your employment history and education.

★ You will receive a PPP registration form. Don't leave without it.

★ The registration form will let you know which positions you can be matched to.

Program S HRO Contacts

Below is a partial list of human resources specialists who provide Program S registration for military spouses. This is a list for USN and USMC. We could not find a list for Army or USCG. This list was provided on June of 2017 and could change! There is NO central location for all of the Program S HRO specialists at this moment for all military bases in the U.S.

To find the Program S HRO at your installation, ask your employment readiness or transition service counselors for the name of the current HRO specialist who provides Program S registration.

OCHR SERVICE CENTERS
PPP TEAM PROGRAM COORDINATORS
POC LISTING

OCHR NORFOLK (EAST)			
CHRISTA CAPONE		757-396-7970	christa.capone@navy.mil
MONICA BROWN		757-203-0279	monica.e.brown@navy.mil
PAULETTE BRAWNER		757-203-0224	paulette.brawner@navy.mil
NINA DRUMMOND		757-396-7034	nina.m.drummond@navy.mil
RHONDA MCGEE		757-396-7599	ronda.mccree@navy.mil
OCHR PHILADELPHIA (NORTHEAST)			
KEVIN SCHUMAN		215-697-0354	kevin.schuman@navy.mil
ALICE BERKOWITZ		215-697-0116	alice.berkowitz@navy.mil
BARBARA FARAGILI		215-697-0126	barbara.faragalli@navy.mil
MYRNA FRAGERMAN	MSP	215-697-0418	myrna.frajerman@navy.mil
DENNIS WENKE		215-697-0361	dennis.wenke@navy.mil
BEVERLY LEMON	DORS	215-697-0336	beverly.lemon@navy.mil
OCHR SAN DIEGO (SOUTHWEST)			
PATRICIA CARTE	A-F	858-577-5667	patricia.carte@navy.mil
MYIRA RAMIREZ	G-L	858-577-5665	myira.ramirez@navy.mil
TERRIE STINTSMAN	M-O	858-577-5728	terri.stintsman@navy.mil
DOM KIMBROUGH	P-S	858-577-5739	dom.kimbrough@navy.mil
CAROLYN HONORE	T-Z	858-577-5690	carolyn.honore@navy.mil
VERONICA DURAN	MSP A-D	858-577-5690	veronica.duran1@navy.mil
GINA MOORE	MSP E-M	858-577-5665	gina.moore1@navy.mil
ALEJANDRA ANAYA	MSP N-S	858-577-5667	alejandra.naya@navy.mil
LADON MOSES	MSP T-Z	858-577-5638	ladon. moses1@navy.mil
OCHR SILVERDALE (NORTHWEST)			
JULIE FRITTS		360-315-8054	julie.fritts@navy.mil
RUTH BRADBURY		360-315-8228	ruth.bradbury@navy.mil
GERI DEMOSS		360-315-8141	geri.demoss@navy.mil
ANGELA DENIS		360-315-4724	amgela.denis@navy.mil
DEBBIE PALMER		360-315-8057	debbie.palmer@navy.mil
EDITH WHARTON		360-315-8229	edith.wharton@navy.mil
CLAIR ESTRIBOR		360-315-8065	clair.estribor@navy.mil
OCHR STENNIS (SOUTHEAST)			
ANITA HENRY	MSP	228-813-1050	anita.henry@navy.mil
LISA VILLA	Overseas	228-813-1193	lisa.villa@navy.mil

Eligibility Questionnaire

Name: ▮▮▮   **Date:** ▮▮▮

Contact Phone #: ▮▮▮

Email: ▮▮▮

Spouses accompanying their military sponsor on a Permanent Change of Station (PCS) move must meet all the following conditions (except #6*).

1) Are you a U.S. citizen?

   ☐ Yes   ☐ No

2) Has your sponsor been serving on active duty for more than 180 consecutive days (6 months)?

   ☐ Yes   ☐ No

3) Did your spouse receive PCS orders to a different commuting area, which authorizes dependent travel? Note: If it is an unaccompanied tour that states sequential assignment orders and you relocate there, then you may be eligible. PCS orders in conjunction with retirement or separation are not eligible for PPP Program S.

   ☐ Yes   ☐ No

4) Were you married to your sponsor on or before the date of the PCS orders?

   ☐ Yes   ☐ No

5) Have you relocated to the new duty station specified on the PCS orders?

   ☐ Yes   ☐ No

   Former Duty Station: ▮▮▮

   Sponsor's New Duty Station: ▮▮▮

   Military Spouse's Current Location: ▮▮▮

   Sponsor's Report Date to New Duty Station: ▮▮▮

6) Have you ever held a federal service position before?*

   ☐ Yes   ☐ No

Additional Notes: ▮▮▮

_____

_____

Eligible for MSP PPP?   ☐ Yes   ☐ No   PPP Initials: _____
(To be filled out by PPP Team)

Improve Your Program S Registry

Your Program S Registration Can Be Improved!

Remember, more option codes and grade levels on your Program S registration will help you match more job announcements in the DOD announcement database.

If you feel that you should be matched to more option codes, occupational series, or grades, improve your resume and return.

Bobbi's Resume Updates Improved Her Score!

Bobbi's original resume was scored for four occupational series with only three Option Codes. She was hoping for more occupational series and Option Codes. Bobbi decided to go back with a longer resume with more specific skills to seek more Option Codes and series, so that she could be eligible for more matches for positions in the Ft. Meade, Maryland area.

See Bobbi's first Program S registration on page 27. After rewriting her resume, Bobbi's Program S registration qualified her as match for the following (new Option Codes and series in pink):

★ 0301, GS-9: FSP, NOA, **BUD, COR, TRB**

★ **1712, GS-7: NOA**

★ 0101 GS-7 to 9: EAP, FSP

★ 0186 GS-7: NOA

★ 0303 GS-7: FSP

-- EXPERIENCE --		FROM		TO
		201402		201504
		200911		201302
-- SKILLS --	PG	SER	III	LO
	GS	*0101*	*09*	*09*
		Options:EAP FSP		
	GS	*0186*	*07*	*07*
		Options:NOA		
	GS	*0301*	*09*	*09*
		Options:FSP NOA BUD COR TRB		
	GS	*0303*	*07*	*07*
		Options:FSP		
	GS	*1712*	*07*	*07*
		Options:NOA		

Star 6

PPP Match Notification

This is a very exciting email. You could receive an email from a human resources specialist telling you that you are MATCHED for a specific position. This is NOT a job offer, but there is a MATCH.

* Registering HRO notifies you if you are matched or selected.
* To accept a Program S position you MUST be in the position before you move to your next PCS location.
* You can only receive one continuing (permanent) position job offer per PCS.
* If you reject this offer, you cannot be offered another one.
* You may receive unlimited appointments to non-continuing positions.

Sample Match Email - PLEASE NOTE: This is NOT a job offer.

I am contacting you because it is my understanding that you are registered in the Priority Placement Program (PPP) (Program S-Military Spouse). Your registration was a potential match to a Social Services Assistant, GS-0186-08, position at Schofield Barracks, HI. During your preliminary PPP consultation, you should have been told that you are required to have a current resume in Application Manager. When a registrant matches against a PPP requisition, the registrant will be contacted and directed to submit an application package through USAJOBS (http://www.usajobs.gov/) including responses to the questionnaire associated with the recruitment action. If it is not feasible for you to complete the application process online, you may provide a completed 1203FX via whatever means is available (e.g., scan and email, fax, provide in person).

The Social Services Assistant announcement (Announcement # NCMD156124361346945) is scheduled to open on Tuesday, March 10, 2015 and will close on Thursday, March 12, 2015. It is your responsibility to apply for this position. According to Chapter 14, Section C.4.b. of the DOD PPP Operations Manual, spouses who decline to participate in established competitive recruitment procedures, such as submitting resumes or responding to assessment questionnaires, will lose their eligibility for continued registration in the Military Spouse Program.

Sample Match Email

"As a result of your Priority Placement Program (PPP) registration, you have been identified as a match for an Information Referral & Follow Up Program Manager position, GS-0101-09 position at USAG-HI, IMCOM, Directorate of Morale Welfare & Recreation, Army Community Services Division on Oahu Island, HI. The vacancy announcement is already closed, but you are currently showing as an applicant who has applied for this vacancy already; therefore, you are not required to apply."

42   The Stars Are Lined Up for Military Spouses

Apply for Jobs on USAJOBS

Star 7

Program S works with USAJOBS! Program S and USAJOBS are integrated to match positions to your Program S registration.

You must apply for jobs to be considered:

★ Referral through Program S is the only means by which eligible, immediately appointable spouses will receive preference for competitive service positions in the US.

★ You can apply before the job closes, or after the job closes if you are contacted about a MATCH.

★ You MUST apply if you are contacted in order to stay in the Program S.

Bobbi's Matches

These DOD positions would match Bobbi's Program S registration. These positions are GS-0300 series, grade level 7/9, and open to FEDERAL EMPLOYEES. Bobbi could apply for these positions on USAJOBS.

Administrative Support Assistant (OA)

DEFENSE HEALTH AGENCY

Agency Contact Information

📍 1 vacancy - Bethesda, MD

Work Schedule is Full-Time - Permanent

Opened Wednesday 5/17/2017
(6 day(s) ago)

🕐 Closes Tuesday 5/23/2017
(0 day(s) away)

Salary Range
$44,941.00 to $58,428.00 / Per Year

Series & Grade
GS-0303-7/7

Supervisory Status
No

Who May Apply
Federal Employees; VEOA; Schedule A; Military Spouses

Control Number
469912200

Job Announcement Number
NCJT178386062133

Administrative Support Specialist

DEFENSE INFORMATION SYSTEMS AGENCY

Agency Contact Information

1 vacancy in the following location:

📍 Fort Meade, MD

Work Schedule is Full Time - Permanent

Opened Friday 5/12/2017
(11 day(s) ago)

🕐 Closes Thursday 5/25/2017
(2 day(s) away)

Salary Range
$44,941.00 to $86,460.00 / Per Year

Series & Grade
GS-0301-07/11

Promotion Potential
11

Supervisory Status
No

Who May Apply
Federal Career/Career-Conditional employees, Transfer, Reinstatement Eligibles, 30% Disabled Veterans, Veterans' Recruitment Appointment (VRA) eligibles, Veterans Employment opportunities Act (VEOA) and other individuals eligible under special appointment authorities

Control Number
469731900

Apply for Other Jobs—
Not Just DOD Jobs

Apply for non-DOD jobs as well, even though Program S does not apply. These positions below are U.S. Citizen positions and will have veterans' preference applied.

Executive Assistant to Court Executives

U.S. COURTS

Agency Contact Information

📍 1 vacancy - Baltimore, MD

Work Schedule is Full-Time - Permanent

Opened Thursday 5/18/2017
(5 day(s) ago)

🕐 Closes Thursday 6/1/2017
(9 day(s) away)

Salary Range
$43,960.00 to $78,703.00 / Per Year

Series & Grade
CL-0303-25/26

Promotion Potential
26

Who May Apply
United States Citizens

Control Number
470182200

Job Announcement Number
DE-10011971-17-CB

Administrative Support Clerk (OA) ZS-0303-II/Administrative Support Assistant (OA) ZS-0303-III

NATIONAL INSTITUTE OF STANDARDS AND TECHNOLOGY

Agency Contact Information

MANY vacancies in the following location:

📍 Gaithersburg, MD

Work Schedule is Full-time - Permanent

Opened Wednesday 5/17/2017
(6 day(s) ago)

🕐 Closes Tuesday 5/23/2017
(0 day(s) away)

Salary Range
$28,886.00 to $58,329.00 / Per Year

Series & Grade
ZS-0303-02/03

Promotion Potential
04

Supervisory Status
No

Who May Apply
All qualified U.S. citizens

Control Number
470001700

Job Announcement Number
NISTOHRM-2017-0016

Save a Search for Job Matches

Star 8

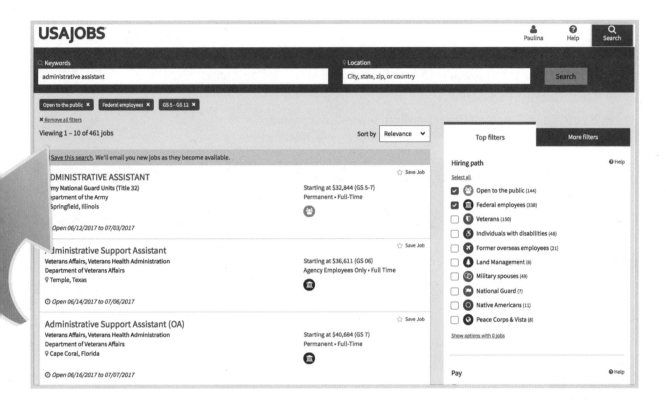

You can also search on your own for qualifying positions and contact HRO if you find one. Here are the steps to follow to set up your SAVED SEARCH:

★ Sign into your USAJOBS account. Only signed in users can save their search.

★ Start a job search by entering a keyword or location in the search box and click Search.

★ Narrow your results using filters.

★ Click Save this search on the search results page located above the search results. This link is hard to find, so follow the arrow above!

★ Name your search—this will help you manage your saved searches.

★ Choose how often you want to get notified. We recommend daily if you're looking for very specific jobs since some jobs can open and close within a week. If you select daily, you'll receive one email per day IF new jobs have been posted that match your criteria in the last 24 hours.

★ Click Save.

Star 9

Follow Up on USAJOBS

USAJOBS includes a great tracking page where you can see your job application status and results.

★ Check your notice of results to see the status of your job application
★ Goal: Get BEST QUALIFIED
★ If you are NOT getting Best Qualified, rework your resume!

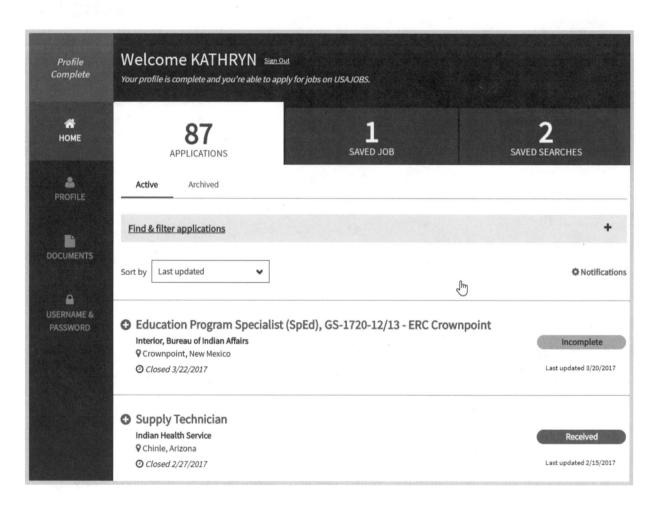

Get Best Qualified

Star **10**

In order for your Program S and USAJOBS application to MATCH, you must be Best Qualified for the position. Be sure to score the application Questionnaire the highest possible, so that the HR specialist can see a MATCH between your resume and one of the Program S job announcements. It will be your number one goal to get Best Qualified and/or Referred for positions.

What Happens if I Get Best Qualified?

★ If you are found "BEST QUALIFIED," your resume will move into the selection pool and all other competitive applicants will be blocked (non-competitive applicants do not get blocked).

★ Management may choose to select a non-competitive applicant or an applicant from an alternative recruitment source (such as VRA, Schedule A person with disabilities) rather than a Program S spouse.

★ A higher priority candidate may be selected instead. Priority 1 and 2 registrants (e.g., DOD civilian employees adversely affected by base closure, realignment, or reduction-in-force) get selected first, then Priority S (Program S).

★ If there is more than one Priority S applicant, the selecting official may select either.

★ If there are no Priority 1 or 2 candidates, a Program S spouse will be selected UNLESS the selecting official decides to select from within the organization.

★ Veterans' preference does not apply.

Ideas for standing out with a MATCH email from HRO:

★ Upload letters of reference from previous employers.

★ Strategically volunteer at organizations where you wish to work.

★ When reporting to the installation, introduce yourself to organizations where you wish to work.

★ If you are a current federal employee, see if your current manager will contact his or her counterpart about your impending arrival.

Interviews

If the results of interviews are not factored into rating and ranking, interviews are NOT allowed. However, if personal interviews are being used as an integral part of the process, managers may choose to interview "Best Qualified" spouses.

So, your resume really must speak for you!

PPP-S Narrative Resumes:
Three Before and After Case Studies

Case Study #1: Jennifer Morris
MATCHED WITH FIRST PPP RESUME!

PPP Match Notification Email

Jennifer Morris,

Your resume has matched the following vacancy being recruited for by this office.

TITLE: MANAGEMENT ASSISTANT(OFFICE AUTOMATION)
PP/SERIES/GRADE: GS-0344-07
ORGANIZATIONAL NAME: AFLCMC/WLNA
DUTY LOCATION: Robins AFB GA
OPEN/CLOSING DATE: 23-27 JAN 2017 ANNOUNCEMENT LINK:
https://www.usajobs.gov/GetJob/ViewDetails/463004200

Failure to comply with the established recruitment procedures or your refusal to participate in the competitive process may result in lack of consideration for the position and possible removal from Program S.

Please remember to upload a copy of your sponsor's PCS Orders to your application when applying to the vacancy announcement. A copy of the PCS Orders is a required supporting document for your military spouse eligibility when applying via USAJOBs.

Thank You,
David P. Smith, Sr.
Human Resources Assistant, DP2YWA2
AFPC Staffing OL-WPAFB
Air Force Personnel Center
2000 Allbrook Dr., Bldg 2
Wright-Patterson AFB, OH 45433

After Resume: Jennifer Morris

Program S and USAJOBS Federal Resume Targeting Admin and HR Assistant

Jennifer Morris

Warner Robins, GA 31088 US
Mobile: 000-000-0000 - Ext:
Email: email@email.com

Availability:

Job Type: Permanent, Presidential Management Fellows, Recent Graduates, Multiple Appointment
Types, Internships
Work Schedule: Full-Time

Desired locations:

United States - GA - Warner Robins

Work Experience:

Brown Mackie College- Albuquerque
10500 Copper Ave
Albuquerque, NM   87123 United States

09/2010 - 10/2011
Salary: 27,040.00 USD Per Year
Hours per week: 40

> Series: 0201 Human Resources
> Option Codes: HRD, STF

Records Assistant/ Human Resource Assistant

Duties, Accomplishments and Related Skills:

RECRUITMENT AND PLACEMENT SUPPORT: Conducted new hire orientation, and answered employee
questions relating to various payroll, benefits and HR issues. Assisted with special events and projects
such as student open house, annual benefits enrollment, etc. as needed.

STUDENT, PERSONNEL AND ACCREDITING AGENCY RECORD KEEPING: Updated and maintained
academic files for over 300 current and former students. Created, updated and maintained personnel
and accrediting agency files for over 50 employees. Achieved zero errors on personnel and accrediting
files from Accrediting Council for Independent Colleges and Schools (ACICS) inspection. Contributed to
the zero errors on academic files for the Registrar Department during ACICS inspection.

OFFICE AUTOMATION SOFTWARE: Utilized office automation software to provide Registrar and Human
Resource services as they relate to clerical and administrative support functions. Entered student

attendance, course registration, course scheduling, input final grades and daily distribution of attendance reports to management. Processed incoming high school and college transcripts, and submitted college transcripts for transfer credit review.

ORAL AND WRITTEN COMMUNICATION: Provided customer service to students, faculty, staff, and external inquiries in person, over the telephone, and through email correspondence.

Supervisor: John Mack (333-333-3333 ext. 11)
Okay to contact this Supervisor: Yes

Brown Mackie College-Albuquerque
10500 Copper Ave
Albuquerque, NM 87123 United States

01/2010 - 09/2010
Salary: 20,800.00 USD Per Year
Hours per week: 40

Receptionist

Series: 0301 and 0318
Option Codes: COR, OAA

Duties, Accomplishments and Related Skills:

VERBAL AND WRITTEN COMMUNICATION: Greeted persons entering establishment, determined nature and purpose of visit, and directed or escorted them to specific destinations. Generated all permanent academic and financial aid student files and gathered computer generated records daily. Verified all files created adhered to state, federal and accreditation regulations. Designed and prepared all front office documents used to sign in guests and track phone and online/website inquiries. Generated and mailed student acceptance letters and reminders to new students and maintained copies in permanent academic files. Prepared and distributed daily and weekly reports to Admissions regarding future class start information.

OFFICE AUTOMATION SOFTWARE AND EQUIPMENT: Operated 8-line telephone switchboard to answer, screen, or forward calls; provide information; and take messages. Tracked student academic placement testing scores for Admissions Department. Transmitted information or documents to customers using phone, email, mail, or facsimile machine. Used system to maintain a current record of staff members' availability and current location.

TRAINING: Trained all part-time receptionists on front office duties. Assisted new Admission Advisors with accurately completing new student enrollment documents.

Supervisor: Tara Harvey (333-333-3333 ext. 10)
Okay to contact this Supervisor: Yes

CiCi's Pizza Buffet
4770 Montgomery Blvd NE D104
Albuquerque, NM 87109 United States

> Series: 0343 Mgt and Program Analyst
> Option Code: PHR

02/2009 - 01/2010
Salary: 27,040.00 USD Per Year
Hours per week: 40

Certified Shift Manager

Duties, Accomplishments and Related Skills:

MANAGEMENT: Managed a team of up to 15 employees per shift. Oversaw all areas of the restaurant and made final decisions on matters of importance to guest service in absence of the General Manager. Scheduled employee shifts and made adjustments when needed. Resolved guest complaints, taking any and all appropriate actions to turn dissatisfied guests into return guests. Resolved interpersonal conflict between employees and or shift managers.

RECRUITMENT AND TRAINING: Interviewed potential employees and made recommendations to General Manager for final decision. Trained and provided direction to employees regarding operational and procedural requirements or issues.

QUALITY CONTROL AND INVENTORY: Maintained product quality and cleanliness. Inventoried goods to ensure we had an adequate amount for the week. Ordered goods whenever levels were low.

FINANCIAL: Completed morning bank deposit and obtained adequate cash and change for the business day. Allocated the accurate amount of money to each register before assigning an employee to the drawer. Maintained registers by skimming drawers hourly to deter and minimize internal and external theft.

Supervisor: Adrian Glover (505-505-5050)
Okay to contact this Supervisor: Yes

McDonalds
1100 Pennsylvania St SE
Albuquerque, NM 87117 United States

11/2007 - 02/2009
Salary: 13,000.00 USD Per Year
Hours per week: 25

Shift Manager

Series: 0340 Program Management
Option Code: PHR

Duties, Accomplishments and Related Skills:

MANAGEMENT- Managed a team of 15-20 employees per shift to ensure quality of service. Resolved guest complaints, taking any and all appropriate actions to turn dissatisfied guests into return guests.

TRAINING AND QUALITY CONTROL: Trained and developed team members' skills and placed them in areas where they excelled. Supervised personnel to ensure that employees were following proper safety and food preparation procedures. Updated employee time sheets and food safety logs.

FINANCIAL: Verified monies in safe and registers to ensure that the accurate amount is accounted for and documented in system. Allocated the accurate amount of money to each register before assigning an employee to a drawer. Maintained registers by skimming drawers hourly to deter and minimize internal and external theft.

Education:

Ashford University-Forbes School of Business Clinton, IA United States
Bachelor's Degree 07/2016
GPA: 3.97 of a maximum 4.00
Major: Business Administration **Honors:** Summa Cum Laude

Affiliations:

Sigma Beta Delta Honor Society – Member

Golden Key International Honour Society -Member

Alpha Sigma Lambda Honor Society - Member

References:

Name	Employer	Title	Phone	Email
John Mack (*)			333-333-3333	
Tara Harvey(*)			333-333-3333	
Adrian Glover(*)			505-505-5050	

(*) Indicates professional reference

Before Resume: Jennifer Morris

Popular bullet format not targeted toward any position

Jennifer Morris

Warner Robins, GA 31088
000-000-0000
Jmorris101@email.com

OBJECTIVE

A performance-driven achiever with exemplary organizational and time management skills, along with a high degree of detail orientation is seeking an entry level to mid-level management position within a company that promotes career advancement and professional growth.

EDUCATION

ASHFORD UNIVERSITY-FORBES SCHOOL OF BUSINESS Clinton, Iowa

B.A. Business Administration, July 2016
- Summa Cum Laude
- Graduate courses:
  - BUS 600- Management Communications with Technology Tools
  - BUS 610- Organizational Behavior

PROFESSIONAL EXPERIENCE

Brown Mackie College **Albuquerque, New Mexico**
Records Assistant/Human Resource Assistant *Sep 2010 – Oct 2011*
- Updated and maintained academic files for over 300 current and former students
- Entered student attendance and distributed attendance reports to management on a daily basis
- Assisted in student orientation, registration, course scheduling, inputted final grades, and preparation for next quarter
- Processed incoming high school and college transcripts, and submitted college transcripts for transfer credit review
- Created, updated and maintained personnel and accrediting agency files for over 50 employees
- Achieved zero errors on personnel and accrediting files from Accrediting Council for Independent Colleges and Schools (ACICS) inspection
- Contributed to the zero errors on academic files for the Registrar Department during ACICS inspection
- Conducted new hire orientation, and answered employee questions relating to various payroll, benefits and HR issues
- Assisted with special events and projects such as student open house, annual benefits enrollment, etc. as needed
- Provided customer service to students, faculty, staff, and external inquiries at the Registrar window and over the telephone

Brown Mackie College **Albuquerque, New Mexico**
Receptionist *Jan 2010 – Sep 2010*
- Greeted persons entering establishment, determined nature and purpose of visit, and directed or escorted them to specific destinations
- Generated all permanent academic and financial aid student files as well as computer generated records daily
- Verified all files created adhered to state, federal and accreditation regulations
- Designed and prepared all front office documents used to sign in guests and track phone and online website inquiries
- Generated student acceptance letters and reminders
- Tracked student academic placement testing scores for Admissions Advisors
- Transmitted information or documents to customers using computer, mail, or facsimile machine
- Kept a current record of staff members' availability and current location
- Generated and mailed all letters to incoming students and maintained copies in permanent academic files
- Assisted the Admission advisors with preparing for each new start date with new student listing and student badges
- Prepared and distributed daily and weekly reports to Admissions regarding future class start information
- Trained part time receptionists on all front office duties
- Operated telephone switchboard to answer, screen, or forward calls, provided information, and took messages

CiCi's Pizza Buffet   **Albuquerque, New Mexico**
Certified Shift Manager   *Feb 2009 – Jan 2010*
➢ Managed a team of up to 15 employees per shift
➢ Oversaw all areas of the restaurant and made final decisions on matters of importance to guest service in absence of the General Manager
➢ Scheduled employee shifts and made adjustments when needed
➢ Resolved guest complaints, taking any and all appropriate actions to turn dissatisfied guests into return guests
➢ Maintained product quality and cleanliness
➢ Trained and provided direction to employees regarding operational and procedural requirements or issues
➢ Allocated the accurate amount of money to each register before assigning an employee to it
➢ Completed morning bank deposit and obtained adequate cash and change for the business day
➢ Maintained registers by skimming drawers hourly to deter and minimize internal and external theft

McDonalds   **Albuquerque, New Mexico**
Shift Manager   *Nov 2007 – Feb 2009*
➢ Managed a team of 15-20 employees per shift to ensure quality of service
➢ Supervised personnel to ensure that employees were following proper safety and food preparation procedures
➢ Tracked store's inventory and
➢ Verified monies in safe and registers to ensure that the accurate amount is accounted for and documented in system
➢ Trained and developed team members' skills and placed them in areas where they excelled
➢ Allocated the accurate amount of money to each register before assigning an employee to it
➢ Maintained registers by skimming drawers hourly to deter and minimize internal and external theft
➢ Updated employee time sheets and food safety logs

United States Army   **Fort Jackson, South Carolina**
Administrative Specialist   *Jan 2001 – Mar 2004*
➢ Greeted visitors or callers and handled their inquiries or directed them to the appropriate person according to their needs
➢ Operated multi-line phone system and provided information to callers, took messages, and transferred calls
➢ Updated and maintained paper and electronic filing systems for records, correspondence, and other material
➢ Composed, typed, and distributed meeting notes, routine correspondence, and reports
➢ Maintained scheduling and leave for unit personnel
➢ Ordered and dispensed unit supplies
➢ Distributed incoming mail or other materials and responded to routine letters

SKILLS

➢ Interpersonal Communication
➢ Intercultural Awareness
➢ Time Management
➢ Adaptability
➢ Leadership
➢ Organizational Skills
➢ Client relations

AFFILIATIONS

➢ Member of Sigma Beta Delta Honor Society
➢ Golden Key International Honour Society
➢ Alpha Sigma Lambda Honor Society

Part Two

Matched and Hired!

Case Study #2: Lori-Anne Romeo

"After many years of trying, with many thanks to your firms' professional services, I finally landed a federal job! The position came by way of the Spouse PPP and it has been just a wonderful journey. My official start date was 28 Nov 2015 on Altus AFB after a PCS move.

In making the transition I took a massive pay cut, but with no regrets."

After Resume: Lori-Anne Romeo

Program S and USAJOBS Federal Resume

LORI-ANNE ROMEO

10224 Virginia Lane
Virginia Beach, VA 23464
(703) 444-4444
LorianneR@gmail.com

Series: 0501 Financial Admin
Option Code: FSY

PROFESSIONAL EXPERIENCE

BANKING CENTER MANAGER V; VICE PRESIDENT, 3/2008 to Present
PNC Bank
1000 Virginia Way, Chesapeake, VA 23320
Salary: $82,000 per year; 45 Hours per week
Supervisor: Kathy Moore (757) 666-6666, may be contacted

MANAGE CONSUMER BANKING OPERATIONS for a PNC branch with $92M in assets. Plan, direct, and implement strategies to ensure the effective delivery and management of consumer, retail, and commercial loans; and financial products and services. Conduct ongoing budgetary, expense, and Profit and Loss (P+L) review to ensure effective funds control and oversight. Apply performance standards to evaluate the effectiveness, efficiency, and regulatory compliance of financial programs and functions.

RECONCILE GENERAL LEDGER (GL) ACCOUNTS: Leverage professional accounting skills to review and reconcile multiple GL accounts, daily. Use data retrieval software to access financial information in the mainframe system. Review and reconcile consumer loans, expenses, operating losses, and other service-related fees. Review and verify daily funds and transaction reports, foreign currency transactions, cost variances, and other GL transactional data to pinpoint overages, shortages, large cash differences, or discrepancies. Track and analyze the personnel budget to ensure payroll is correctly calculated.

CONDUCT FINANCIAL, OPERATIONAL, COMPLIANCE, AND PERFORMANCE AUDITS: Develop methods and techniques to conduct a variety of audits and audit risk assessments in accordance with Generally Accepted Auditing and Accounting Standards (GAAS/GAAP). Test and examine accounting systems and records, costs representations, and internal controls to ensure compliance with specifications and regulatory requirements. Identify and correct internal control weaknesses. Apply audit criteria to verify fixed, variable, and direct/indirect costs.

Series: 0510 Accounting
Option Codes: ADT, COQ, INE, SYA

DEVELOP AUDIT AND FINANCIAL REPORTS: Prepare audit working papers and reports for management with audit determinations, recommendations, and conclusions. Identify deficiencies, violations, and non-compliance. Assess financial performance through review of operational control records, GL accounting reports, and sales. Prepare weekly reports for senior management and recommend strategies for improving profit performances and reducing costs.

Series: 0340 Program Management
Option Code: PHR

SUPERVISE EIGHT FINANCIAL SERVICES STAFF, including one Client Service Manager. Establish performance goals; evaluate performance bi-annually. Promote ongoing professional training. Lead by example and motivate staff using one-on-one coaching and team meetings. Award merit increases to top performers. Implement work schedules to optimize service levels to customers.

DEMONSTRATE EFFECTIVE COMMUNICATIONS SKILLS, ORALLY AND IN WRITING: Communicate daily with clients, area business managers, team members, and senior management. Promote exemplary customer service to strengthen retention and expand customer base. Develop and lead presentations, seminars, and other promotions to educate customers on consumer banking services.

Series: 0201 Admin
Option Code: COR

TEAM LEADERSHIP / BUSINESS DEVELOPMENT: Develop, execute, and lead integrated sales, customer relationship management, and credit strategies to achieve target revenue, expense, and service goals. Drive portfolio growth and cultivate strong customer relationships through effective cross-selling. Coach teams in effective techniques to increase customer sales.

REGULATORY SUBJECT MATTER EXPERT (SME): Ensure adherence with and provide technical guidance to staff on financial and consumer protection regulations, including the Fair Housing, Bank Secrecy, and Home Mortgage Disclosure Acts. Continually assess financial programs and functions to assure regulatory compliance. Identify "red flags" to mitigate loss and reduce fraud.

LEVERAGE TECHNICAL PROFICIENCY IN FINANCIAL SYSTEMS, SPREADSHEETS, DATA MANAGEMENT, AND WORD PROCESSING SOFTWARE to monitor and execute financial activities; perform accounting, financial analysis, and audit functions; and to prepare reports and communications.

Series: 1102 Business and Industry
Option Code: COL

MANAGE $25M LOAN PORTFOLIO that includes small business, residential and commercial real estate loans and lines of credit. Perform credit and economic analyses. Source, originate, and manage the loan process from origination to funding.

KEY ACCOMPLISHMENTS:
+ Performed workforce analysis and realigned staffing levels to meet customer needs during peak periods, which reduced overtime costs to zero—a costs savings of $2000 per month.
+ Drove a 20% improvement in service, year over year, through proactive resolution of issues.
+ Instrumental in driving $4M growth in deposits, year over year, for 3,500 households through astute financial and operational oversight and effective personnel management.
+ Consistently exceed personal performance goals and bank production goals for sales, referrals, and revenue production. Ranked in the top 30% of all PNC teammates for sales/referral production in 2011-2013; the team I led was ranked in the top 45%. Led branch that generated $100,000 in investment revenue and $5M in mortgage loans in 2013.

BANKING CENTER MANAGER IV / ASSISTANT VICE PRESIDENT, 02/2007 to 02/2008
Key Bank
7500 Peninsula Way, Pensacola, FL 32504
Salary $60,000; 40 Hours per week
Supervisor: Pat Thompson (850) 888-8888

> Series:0511 Finance
> Option Code: FIN

MANAGED BANKING OPERATIONS for a branch with $25M in deposits, a $16M loan portfolio, and seven sales and client services employees. Planned, analyzed, managed, and monitored deposit and loan balances, mortgage lending operations, banking products and services, and merchant services and investment sales. Accountable for achieving targeted goals and objectives through effective P+L, business development, financial administration, and personnel management. Provided astute financial and strategic operations leadership to drive revenue growth, strengthen customer relationships, and enhance staff productivity.

FINANCIAL AND PERFORMANCE AUDITS; GENERAL LEDGER ACCOUNTING:
Performed a broad range of financial, accounting, and reporting functions to assess operational efficiency and accuracy, internal controls; and to mitigate risk and loss from fraud. Leveraged knowledge of Generally Accepted Accounting Principles (GAAP) and Generally Accepted Auditing Standards (GAAS) to plan and perform surprise and scheduled audits of teller cash counts.

UTILIZED CONVENTIONAL AUDITING METHODS AND TECHNIQUES to analyze multiple GL accounts including shortages and overages reports, fraud and non-fraud losses, safe deposit boxes, fee income and expenses, loan fees, lost monetary instruments, and teller daily balancing journals. Reviewed daily sales plans, daily debriefs, phone and in person consultations with clients. Monitored the large transaction report daily, to reduce attrition of deposit dollars. Audited client accounts and identified errors in payments or unauthorized transactions. Wrote audit reports, with audit findings and determinations, for senior management.

Series:0560 Budget Analyst
Option Code: WCF

FINANCIAL ANALYSIS AND BUDGET MANAGEMENT: Analyzed new deposit accounts, new business acquisition, and investment revenue evaluate branch performance. Managed a $50,000 business development budget. Allocated spending to maximize Return on Investment (ROI). Realigned funding, as needed, to adjust to changing priorities and business requirements.

UTILIZED PROFESSIONAL ACCOUNTING KNOWLEDGE AND STRONG PROBLEM SOLVING SKILLS to research and resolve financial issues. Analyzed weekly branch reports on all operational and accounting areas. Evaluated loan fee income, credit report variances, deposit account disputes, sales performance, mortgage lending, income and expenses, and the efficiency and effectiveness of the branch. Outlined findings for senior management with recommendations for corrective actions, cost reductions, and efficiency improvement.

REGULATORY COMPLIANCE: Ensured all banking center operations were compliant with Federal laws and regulations including the Community Reinvestment Act and Truth in Lending Act. Ensured all staff followed corporate banking policy, guidelines, procedures, and consumer regulations to protect the privacy of customer information and financial data.

CUSTOMER SERVICE: Strived to maintain the highest level of customer service while achieving annual retail sales goals. Developed and implemented operational strategies to increase profit margins.

KEY ACCOMPLISHMENTS:
+ Consistently achieved target goals of $5M in new deposits and $3M in new loan production.
+ Drove a 50% increase in the number of credit cards issued to customers by recommending lending staff cross-sell the bank's credit card to every loan client.
+ Took initiative to conduct a thorough review of obligations and expenditures and identified process improvements and operating efficiencies, which resulted in a 25% cost savings and ensured branch operated within budget.

BRANCH MANAGER III / ASSISTANT VICE PRESIDENT, 05/2005 to 02/2007
Community Bank
11- South Martins Way, Pensacola, Fl 32501
Salary $53,000; 40 Hours per week
Supervisor: Henry Boyd, (850) 444-4444

MANAGED BRANCH OPERATIONS AND LED BUSINESS DEVELOPMENT for an Community branch with $23M in deposits and an $18M loan portfolio. Planned and led external business development activities to grow deposits and loan base.

LEVERAGED ADVANCED FINANCIAL AND OPERATIONS ANALYSIS SKILLS and financial industry knowledge to assess credit processes, loan portfolio management, banking regulations, and profitability of banking products. Formed and executed

analyses and identified areas for improvement, development, or inefficiency. Analyzed the risk and feasibility of new products and programs.

PREPARED AND PRESENTED WEEKLY REPORTS TO SENIOR MANAGEMENT. Used Excel to develop analytical and production reports on the strengths, weaknesses, and opportunities in consumer banking.

MANAGED, TRAINED, MENTORED, COACHED, AND DEVELOPED A TEAM of nine sales employees. Trained staff in building customer relationships through effective cross selling of financial services, including trust and investment service, mortgage lending, private banking, and business banking/commercial lending. Resolved employee issues on the branch level, and served as a liaison to Human Resources for more complex issues.

LEVERAGED EXPERT KNOWLEDGE OF FAIR LENDING LAWS, REGULATIONS AND POLICIES TO ENSURE COMPLIANCE with the Home Mortgage Disclosure, Fair Housing, ECO, Community Reinvestment (CRA), Truth in Lending, and Civil Rights Acts, and other applicable regulations. Ensured staff followed established policies and consumer regulations, such as the FACT Act and Privacy of Consumer Information.

RELATIONSHIP MANAGEMENT / COMMUNICATIONS: Relied on strong interpersonal and communication skills to grow and manage banking relationships. Proactive and tenacious in developing new business by fostering strong relationships with existing clients and through referrals. Led outreach to areas businesses to expand commercial loans and accounts. Aggressively developed cross-selling opportunities.

CREATED AND LED POWERPOINT PRESENTATIONS: Relied on strong public speaking skills to lead sales meetings and professional training for staff and managers. Tailored communication to the audience's level of understanding and used different communication methods to deliver clear and concise messages.

USED AUTOMATED SYSTEMS, including Excel, to track financial and operational data.

KEY ACCOMPLISHMENTS:
+ Led nine-person sales team recognized with the 2006 Chairman's Club Award for the first time in four years for superior sales and impeccable operations.
+ Through meticulous accounting analysis and internal audit reviews, identified errors and payments and unauthorized transactions that were referred to the appropriate department for further investigation.

EDUCATION

Master of Science, Management, 2003
Florida Institute of Technology Graduate Center, Pensacola, FL

Bachelor of Business Administration, Marketing, 1998
University of North Florida, Jacksonville, Florida

COURSEWORK, LICENSURES AND CERTIFICATIONS

Securities Licenses, Series 6 and 63; Virginia Life, Health and Variable Annuities

Master's in Management and Bachelor's in Business Administration includes 24
semester hours in Accounting.

ADDITIONAL INFORMATION

PROFESSIONAL PROFILE

SENIOR BANKING MANAGER with 15 years of successful commercial and retail
banking, branch operations management, lending oversight, and staff leadership and
training experience. Cross-functional experience in internal controls auditing, financial
analysis, general ledger accounting, business development, customer relationship
management, strategic planning, and compliance assurance. Expert knowledge of
consumer protection programs; banking procedures, theory, and practice; financial, risk,
cash flow, and loan credit analysis; banking and commercial law; and loan
documentation and underwriting. Record of accomplishment leading internal audits and
spearheading process improvements to strengthen controls and compliance, increase
efficiency, and improve profit performance. Articulate and effective communicator,
presenter, and training leader. Strong writing skills.

SPECIAL NOTE: Military Spouse to US Navy, E7, an active duty service member.

Before Resume: Lori-Anne Romeo

Big Block Resume in USAJOBS Format

LORI-ANNE ROMEO

Virginia Beach Virginia

EDUCATION

Master of Science, Management April 2003
Florida Institute of Technology Graduate Center Patuxent River, Maryland

Bachelor of Business Administration, Marketing December 1998
University of North Florida Jacksonville, Florida

Honors Diploma in Business Administration June 1995
Merit Certificate in Business Administration June 1994
University of Technology Kingston, Jamaica

LICENSE

Virginia Life, Health and Variable Annuities; Series 6 and 63

WORK EXPERINCE

PNC
1000 Virginia Way, Chesapeake Virginia 23320

Banking Center Manager V
Vice President

Managed, generated and serviced profitable business and retail relationships of a $67 million dollar deposit and $25 million dollar loan branch office. Managed the growth of deposits by $4 million dollars. Prepared and interpreted weekly branch reports for senior managements review outlining findings and recommending strategies for corrective action and improvement. Performed clients account analysis and examination to provide recommendation for additional services. Identified errors in payments and potential unauthorized transactions to be referred for immediate correction. Planned and directed the activities of a branch, including the management of 8 exempt and non-exempt employees. Performed workforce planning and analysis by reviewing teammate versus client needs and scheduling accordingly. The activity resulted in the reduction of overtime to zero and an overall monthly savings of approximately $2000 per month. Tracked and updated personnel records in various data bases. Performed and delivered performance reviews for 8 employees on a bi-annual basis. Awarded merit increases as appropriate for employees using performance outcome as the leading factor. Developed standards for branch daily, weekly, monthly and quarterly reporting, service standards and retention of deposit dollars. Ensured the achievement of goals and service standards. Coordinated sales strategies with Area Manager; directed branch sales meetings and demonstrated comprehensive knowledge of retail and business products and services to achieve branch sales goals. Managed the daily execution of service quality which resulted in a 20% improvement year over year.

March 2008-Present
Supervisor- Kathy Moore (757) 666-6666
Salary plus quarterly incentive
45 Hours per week

Key Bank
7500 Peninsula Way, Pensacola Florida 32504

Banking Center Manager IV
Assistant Vice President
Managed all aspects of a $25 million deposit and $16 million loan base banking center sales and service operation. Maintained the highest level of customer service while achieving annual retail sales goals. Prepared and interpreted weekly branch reports for senior managements review outlining findings and recommending strategies for corrective action and improvement. Performed clients account analysis and examination to provide recommendation for additional services. Identified errors in payments and potential unauthorized transactions to be referred for immediate correction. Participated daily in identifying and establishing client account process improvement with the use of monthly statements. Directly managed 7 sales and service personnel including the Customer Service Manager. Devised recruitment strategies and coordinated employee recruitment events. Managed all aspects of bank operations and ensured compliance with federal laws.

February 2007-February 2008
Supervisor- Pat Thompson (850) 888-8888
Salary plus monthly and quarterly incentive
40 Hrs per week

Community Bank
11- South Martins Way, Pensacola Florida 32501

Branch Manager III
Assistant Vice President
Managed a $23 million deposit and $18 million loan branch office with particular emphasis on outside business

development activities both to sustain and grow deposit and loan base for branch. Lead the work team to the achievement of the 2006 Chairman's club award for the first time in four years. Prepared and interpreted weekly branch reports for senior managements review outlining findings and recommending strategies for corrective action and improvement. Acted as a liaison with the Human Resource Department to resolve discrepancies. Performed clients account analysis and examination to provide recommendation for additional services. Identified errors in payments and potential unauthorized transactions to be referred for immediate correction. Managed and developed an effective sales team of 9 employees including the building of customer relationships by referrals to other lines of business including trust and investment service, mortgage lending, private banking and business banking/commercial lending.

Supervisor- Henry Boyd (850) 444-4444
May 2005- February 2007
Salary plus quarterly incentive
40 Hours per week

Bank of America Incorporated
220 West Garden Street Pensacola Florida 32502

Branch Manager III
Bank Officer
Managed, generated and serviced profitable business and retail relationships of a $28 million dollar deposit and an $18 million loan branch office. Prepared and interpreted weekly branch reports for senior managements review outlining findings and recommending strategies for corrective action and improvement. Performed clients account analysis and examination to provide recommendation for additional services. Planned and directed the activities of a branch, including the management of exempt and non-exempt employees. Ensured the achievement of sales goals and service standards. Coordinated sales strategies with Market or Region Manager; directed branch sales meetings and demonstrated comprehensive knowledge of retail and business products and services to achieve branch sales goals.

Assistant Manager III
Financial Service Representative III
Supported the branch manager, coached and mentored employees to achieve sales results. Managed employees to ensure development of staff and coached employee performance issues. Demonstrated excellent service to clients while acting in the best interest of the bank. Established new retail and commercial accounts and enhanced existing relationships by providing financial management planning and execution support. Reconciled financial information pertinent to clients and the bank. Provided assistance to clients seeking loans and performed various administrative duties as assigned. Resolved problems and concerns in a timely manner and provided superior customer service to all clients.

Supervisor- Cate Holt (850) 456-0123
March 1999- May 2005
Salary plus monthly commission and bonus
40 Hours per week

Bank of America
On the Job Trainer
Provided comprehensive on the job training for newly hired Financial Sales Representatives. Coached these employees to ensure a superior level of service in all customer interactions. Evaluated the performance of the trainee and recommended areas of needed concentration upon arrival to assigned branch.

VOLUNTEER EXPERIENCE

Navy Marine-Corp Relief Society- NAS Pensacola

Caseworker
Analyzed client requests for assistance, completed required verifications, budget analysis and reviewed previous casework history. Assessed needs presented and determined final outcome within NMCRS Relief policies assistance with loans, grants, or other services/referrals. Assisted client with identifying alternate solutions to presented problems and made professional referrals to community resources.

Supervisor-Mario Hargrove (850) 456-2345
February 2004- October 2004
6 Hours per week

AWARDS

PNC Edge Achiever 2008 Award, PNC Bank, Hampton Roads Region, Virginia
Community Bank Chairman's Club Award 2006, Community Bank, Pensacola, Florida
PNC Edge Leader 2002 Award, PNC Bank, Greater Washington Region, Maryland
Best Marketing Student 1996 Award Desnoes and Geddes Bottlers Limited, Kingston, Jamaica

Matched and Hired!

Case Study #3: Natalie Richardson
GS-9 Public Affairs Specialist

"I just wanted to let you ladies know, that thanks to your awesome resume skills, I have landed a job! It is a GS-9 position as a public affairs specialist. I will be in charge of all the advertising for the recruiting battalion here in VA. I LOVE YOU GUYS! They hired me based on my resume and questionnaire - they didn't even ask for an interview! Natalie"

After Resume: Natalie Richardson

Program S and Federal Resume for Uploading into USAJOBS—Targeting Public Affairs

Natalie Richardson
2050 Norfolk Way
Fort Lee, VA 23801
(912) 444-4444
Nrichardson1234@gmail.com

WORK EXPERIENCE:

PARTNER/MANAGER   **09/2010 - 02/2011**

BaseCouponConnection.com, 45 Tipton Lane, Fort Stewart, GA 31315
Salary: $2,160 per month, Hours per week: 45
Supervisor: Natalie Richardson (Self), Phone: 999-999-9999, May contact.

MARKETING PROGRAM FOR MILITARY FAMILIES WITH FAMILY MEMBER IN IRAQ. Developed, owned, managed and operated business that sold marketing contracts to local businesses. Marketed "Send It To Your Sweetie" program targeting free services to military families with members in Iraq for shipping, phone messages, and personal delivery of gifts for their loved ones. Met with base command to ensure all regulations and policies were met.

- Accomplishment: Conceptualized a successful program for family members to send gifts and messages to military personnel. More than 2,500 messages were sent through this program in just 6 months. Sold business in less than 6 months for a substantial profit.

COMMUNICATIONS. Wrote business plan and developed all aspects of advertising and marketing. Performed cold calls on business customers and followed up with written proposals. Created and delivered PowerPoint presentations to groups of various sizes. Organized and prepared mailings to families and businesses.

WEBSITE DESIGN: Designed website and prepared spreadsheet to track monthly views and clicks. Due to volume of business, interviewed and hired 3 contractors to assist with billing, designing ads, and updating website.

MANAGER   **06/2005 – 07/2007**

Business Card Wholesalers, 1010 Nethers Lane, Atlanta, GA 30016
Salary: $3,000 per month, Hours per week: 75
Supervisor: Jason Smart, Phone: 666-666-6666, May Contact

CREATIVE PRODUCTION: Sold and created full-color, personalized business cards to small businesses. Planned and organized work; efficiently and effectively processed the sale, design, ordering and delivery of product. Ensured quality control and timeliness for re-orders.

- Established a successful in-home business with local producers of business cards. Contracted with more than 15 vendors and tracked orders for more than 200 customers in two years. Efficiently set up and managed own schedule and schedule for automatic reordering.

CUSTOMER SERVICES: Provided administrative support to customers and vendors. Prepared and sent invoices; collected balances due. Conducted all aspects of accounting.

COMMUNICATION: Corresponded with clients by email and phone; ensured correct grammar, spelling and format. Made cold calls to small businesses – utilized interpersonal skills to develop customer base of 300 businesses within 6 months.

COMPUTER SKILLS: : Utilized typing speed of 45 wpm, Microsoft Suite programs for reports and communication, as well as Photoshop, Illustrator and Corel software to design cards.

Demonstrated strong customer services skills; multi-tasked and worked under pressure and constant deadlines. Maintained customer relations; photographed clients and worked with customers to achieve their desired customized product.

PUBLIC RELATIONS   **02/2004 - 01/2005**

Multi Care Health and Rehab LLC, 1650 Honey Creek Commons, Suite F
Conyers, GA 30013
Salary: $2,300 per month, 40 hours per week
Supervisor: Gina Thomas, Phone: 777-777-7777, May Contact

BUSINESS DEVELOPMENT AND COMMUNICATIONS: Represented chiropractic clinic public relations, made new business contacts, mended old contacts. Developed lasting business relationships with store managers, district managers and their assistants, both inside and outside the office. Scheduled health screenings involving blood pressure, glucose and cholesterol testing. Ensured excellent service. Successfully increased patient roster by an average of 5 new patients per week.

STORE MANAGER   **04/2002 - 02/2004**

Phoebe's Boutique, 1345 Nixon Lane, Lithonia, GA 30038
Salary: $2,580 per month, Hours per week: 40
Supervisor: Marcia Mendez, Phone: 777-777-7777, May Contact

ADMINISTRATION: Performed office and store administration including management of files and official records, training, payroll and reporting. Communicated effectively orally and in writing. Developed, wrote, standardized and regulated customer service procedures, policies and systems.

COMMUNICATIONS: Communicated with diverse customers, vendors and management to increase sales and resolve problems. Greeted and assisted customers with special requests. Trained staff to deliver excellent customer service.

COMPUTER SKILLS: Utilized computer skills to design website and regulate maintenance for user effectiveness. Used Microsoft Word for correspondence and Excel for reports. Ensured accuracy as well as correct grammar, spelling, punctuation and syntax.

MANAGED STAFF AND BUDGET: Planned and organized work for sales staff; managed budgeting for cost effective sales planning; directed all tasks and aspects of controlling, maintaining and rotating inventory. Designed store layout and product presentations.

MARKETING SOLUTIONS: Gathered pertinent data and recognized solutions to initiate and conduct successful storewide marketing campaigns. Controlled and minimized expenses to maximize profit through selected business improvements.

EDUCATION:

National Emergency Medical Technician Intermediate
DeKalb Technical Institute, Covington, GA 30014
GPA: 4.0 of a maximum 4.0, 1 year course.
 Certification November 7, 2001

ADDITIONAL INFORMATION

BILINGUAL:

French:	Speak, Read; Advanced
	Write: Intermediate
Spanish:	Speak, Read, Write: Novice

Extensive international travel; lived abroad in various circumstances.

CERTIFICATION AND LICENSURE
National Emergency Medical Technician Intermediate, Certification November 7, 2001

COMPUTER AND TECHNICAL SKILLS
Computer: Microsoft Word, Microsoft Excel, Word Perfect, Microsoft Publisher, Power Point, Graphic Design: Photoshop, Illustrator, Corel.

Typing speed: 45 WPM

PROFESSIONAL TRAINING
2004, Two Day Public Relations Training Seminar, David Singer Enterprises, Inc., Clearwater, FL 33755
Individual Coaching, Teleconference Training, Public Speaking, Insurance Billing & Coding, Staff Training, How to Book and Deliver Outside Lectures, and Patient Policies.

Before Resume: Natalie Richardson

Bullet Format Targeting Administrative, Database, Tracking, Computers, Customer Services

Natalie Richardson

1050 Norfolk Way / Fort Lee, VA 23801 / (912) 444-4444

OBJECTIVE/GOAL: General Administrative, Clerical and Office Services– 0300/0399-GS-07
Eligible for Noncompetitive Appointment of Certain Military Spouses – PCS Orders Attached

WORK EXPERIENCE:

Base Coupon Connection *Fort Stewart, Georgia*   *Sept. 2010- Feb.. -2011 (Owner)*
OFFERS FROM LOCAL BUSINESSES SERVING THE MILITARY AND THEIR FAMILIES

- Owned and operated BaseCouponConnection.com
- Sold 3, 6, and 12 month contracts to local businesses.
- Responsible for marketing local businesses to military members in Iraq with free shipping, phone messages, and free personal delivery on gifts for their loved ones. (Send It To Your Sweetie)
- Maintained categories for Fort Stewart, GA and Fort Gordon, GA: with sub-categories which included Restaurant guide/reviews, Send It To Your Sweetie and Game Source Forum (for Deployed service members), Coupons, Deals, Freebies and Map It.
- Free for the military and their families to access and use all offers provided from participating local businesses.
- Designed website and all aspects of Advertising/Marketing.

Business Card Wholesalers *Conyers, Georgia month, 2005-2009 (Owner)* Owned and operated Business Card Wholesalers.

- Sold thousands of printing products to small businesses on a daily basis.
- Designed and distributed orders within seven days of every order.
- Conducted all aspects of accounting.
- Maintained customer relations by calling, dropping by and making re-orders within 6 months of previous orders.
- Photographed clients and worked with customers to achieve their desired customized product.
- Currently accepting re-orders and working with customers long-distance.

EDUCATION:

National Emergency Medical Technician Intermediate
DeKalb Technical Institute, Covington, GA 30014
GPA: 4.0 of a maximum 4.0, 1 year course.
Certification November 7, 2001

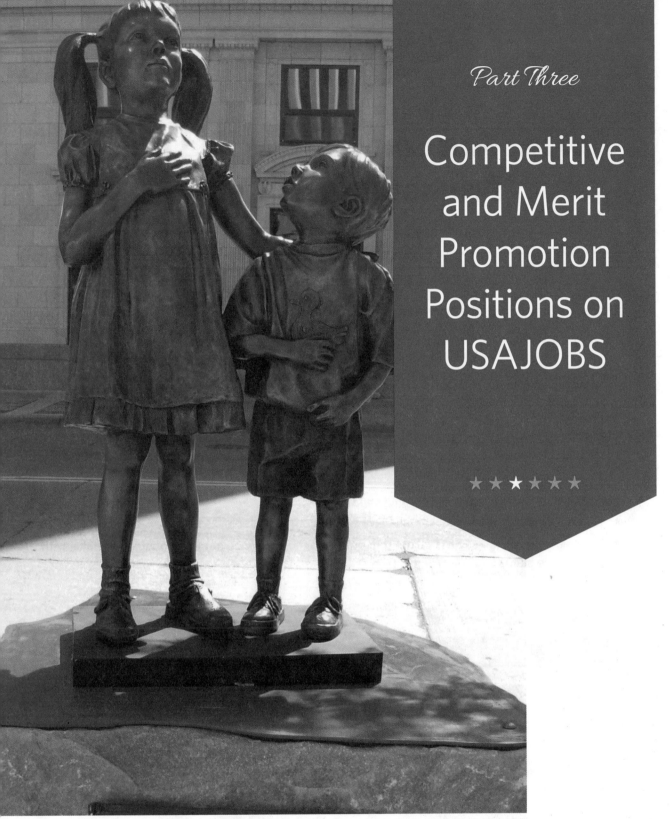

Published with permission by Jams Haire, Ft. Collins, CO.

Competitive and Merit Promotion Positions on USAJOBS

★ ★ ★ ★ ★

"A two-income home will allow my family to weather financial storms due to emergencies and provide additional income to allow us to save since it never fails to rain."

What Are Competitive and Merit Promotion Positions?

Military spouses can apply to both kinds of federal jobs posted on USAJOBS

- ★ "Open to the Public (US Citizen)" jobs are competitive positions.

- ★ "Federal Employee" jobs are merit promotion positions.

Open to the Public (US Citizen) Jobs Are Competitive

- ★ Anyone with U.S. citizenship may apply. You will be competing with other members of the general public.
- ★ You can apply for these jobs if you've never worked for the federal government (or don't have civil service "status").
- ★ Veterans' preference does apply to these positions.
- ★ This is the normal entry route into the civil service for most employees.
- ★ The selecting official may fill the job from outside the civil service or from among candidates with civil service status.

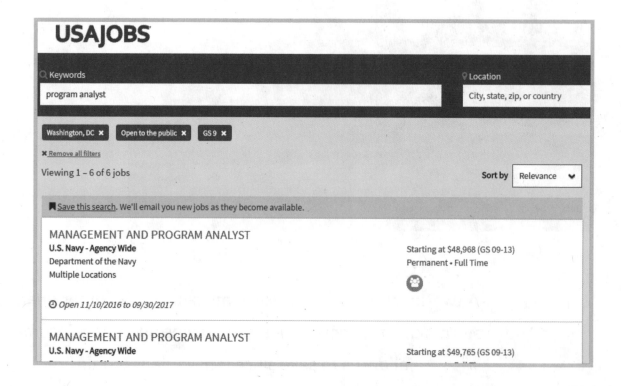

Federal Employee Jobs Are Merit Promotion Positions

★ These announcements are limited to current or former federal employees. You will be competing against other "status" candidates.

★ You will not be competing with members of the general public!

★ Veterans' preference does not apply to these positions.

★ To limit your USAJOBS search to "Merit Promotion" positions, select the "federal employee filter." Also, read the "Who May Apply" section of the job announcement. It will typically state "status candidates" or "merit promotion." Other groups (such as those who may be hired under special hiring authorities) may also be listed - such as military spouses!

Program S and E.O. 13473 military spouses apply for "federal employee" announcements that meet the Program S requirements (e.g., DOD CONUS jobs within commuting distance of your PDS) and match their series/grades. But they may also decide to apply for U.S. Citizen vacancies.

Samples of Job Announcements: "Who May Apply"

Who May Apply
This includes employees on career or career-conditional appointments, individuals eligible for special appointing authorities such as Veterans Employment Opportunity Act, Interagency Career Transition Program/Career Transition Program, Schedule A, and individuals on Interchange Agreements with Other Merit Systems. (such as Military Spouse EO 13473)

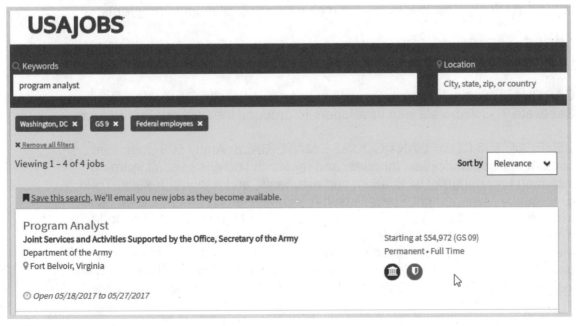

Sample Builder Federal Resume in the Outline Format

KATHRYN L. THOMPSON
655 West Lake Road
Catonsville, MD 21228 US
Day Phone: 907-333-3333 - Ext:
Email: Kathryn.l.thompson@gmail.com
Availability:
Job Type: Permanent, Temporary, Term
Work Schedule: Full-Time, Part-Time, Shift Work, Intermittent, Job Sharing, Multiple Schedules

Desired locations:
United States - CO – Denver United States

Work Experience:
FEMA
1000 Constitution Ave.
Washington DC, DC   20004 United States

01/2013 - Present
Hours per week: 40
INSTRUCTIONAL DESIGN SPECIALIST
Duties, Accomplishments and Related Skills:
DESIGN CURRICULUM AND PLAN LEARNING PRODUCTS:
Consult/collaborate enterprise-wide with management, Headquarters, EEO, Safety, Security, Quality Control, Program Specialists, and contractors in the curriculum design, development and maintenance of plans and programs.

ADOBE E-LEARNING SUITE: Utilize Adobe Connect for current virtual training. Completed training and designing curriculum modules with Adobe.

CAPTIVATE 5 and 7: Design curriculum components with Captivate 5 and Captivate 7. Collaborate with developers to produce the best quality products.

DEVELOP 508-COMPLIANT COURSE MATERIALS: Apply 508-compliant content, format, principles, theories, and research findings in adult learning including knowledge of evaluation, surveys, tests, and analysis results. Train Emergency Management Specialists in a technical environment allows us to focus on the Adult Learning Theory and Behaviorist theory. According to Malcolm Knowles, adults are practical learners and want relatable information. Coordinate the packaging of training materials and revising or developing new courses based on this process. Manipulate graphics and edit course materials, ensuring instructional materials are 508 compliant.

STRUCTURE CLASSROOM AND WEB-BASED COURSE DESIGN by planning, developing, monitoring, evaluating, delivering, and managing one or more curriculum areas utilizing traditional and virtual training. Utilize blended learning in courses. Independently and co-train courses.

ANALYZE TRAINING TASKS: Analyze learning problems, selecting instructional media and methods for learner engagement and applying knowledge of steps to perform tasks associated with training and task analysis. Assist individuals requiring additional performance requirements training on tasks.

CONDUCT TRAINING NEEDS ANALYSIS and research to identify and develop courses, revise course content to reflect changing policy and guidance, legislative and agency emphasis. Demonstrate knowledge of evaluation practices, surveys, and analysis results.

KEY ACCOMPLISHMENTS:

• PROFESSIONAL PROGRAM SPECIALIST. Co-Designer/ Co-Trainer. 80 hours to develop. Professional Development course on Time Management, Goal Setting, Coaching, Mentoring, Steps to Building a Strong Performer, Process Improvement/Problem, Solving, Motivating Self and Others, and Steps to a Strong Performer. Used PowerPoint and Word to create PowerPoint Slides, Instructor Guide, agenda, job aids, and exercises.

• DESIGN VALID AND RELIABLE TESTS: Utilize learning objectives test questions, designed to relate to each corresponding objective. Partner with trainers, developers, participants, Quality Control and the Special Projects Unit to validate courses. Program Specialists assist by piloting new courses and are tested using assessment materials administered to participants, who point out troublesome wording and other difficulties. Program Specialists also assist with discussions of assessment decisions as answers are not necessarily interpreted the same way.

• REVISE COURSES USING KIRKPATRICK TRAINING: Courses are designed using the ADDIE Model (Analyze, Design, Develop, Implement, and Evaluate) and Kirkpatrick's four levels. Kirkpatrick's evaluation is relevant to pre- and post-testing in our training department. The training department continually works toward post-training assessments three or more months following the course.

Johns Hopkins University
1740 Massachusetts Ave NW
Washington DC, DC   20036 United States

01/2011 – 01/2013
Hours per week: 40
CAREER COUNSELOR
Duties, Accomplishments and Related Skills:
DEVELOPED, IMPLEMENTED AND MANAGED MULTI-MILLION DOLLAR
EMPLOYEE DEVELOPMENT PROGRAMS. Established the office of Career
Services at the Hopkins-Nanjing Center Provided career counsel to Chinese and
Non-Chinese Citizens on topics related to choosing a career, job interviewing,
resume writing, networking, and other career-related skills.

PREPARED EMPLOYEES TO WORK AND LEAD IN INTERNATIONAL
ENVIRONMENTS. Managed employer relationships for Johns Hopkins SAIS in
Greater China, building a database with over 750 contacts representing a variety
of public, private, multilateral, and non-profit organizations.

PROFESSIONAL DEVELOPMENT. Conducted weekly workshops to help
students with their professional development.

BUDGET MANAGEMENT. Planned and launched an event with a budget of
roughly $35,000.

INSTRUCTOR. Taught the Professional Development Course at the Hopkins-
Nanjing Center, a four-part module designed to present structure and guidance
to students in their career development.

KEY ACCOMLISHMENTS:
• Managed, budgeted, and launched the Beijing Career Trek, a four-day
experiential trip where approximately 20 students visited various companies and
organizations in Beijing to learn about their operations, strategy, and hiring
needs. Managed and led the Asia Career Trek, a six-day experiential trip where
approximately 20 students visited various companies and organizations in
Shanghai and Hong Kong to learn about their operations, strategy, and hiring
needs. Trek received the highest reviews of any of the 12 JHU SAIS Treks
(2013, 2014, 2015).

• Planned, executed, and administered the Hopkins-Nanjing Center Career Day
2012-2015, a day-long event with approximately 500 participants where students
heard from business leaders regarding their career advice.

USAJOBS Resume Builder:
Store Up to Five Resumes

You can store five different resumes in your USAJOBS account. You can upload your resume or build the resume in the Builder. The human resources specialists prefer the Builder resumes because of the information is organized in one specific format. Your resumes should be named carefully for your target positions.

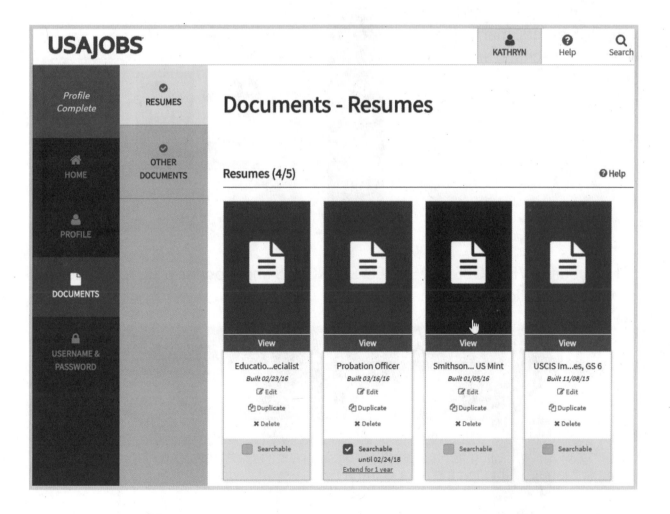

USAJOBS Tips

Be sure to upload your documents ahead, such as your PCS orders, marriage license, transcripts, and DD-214 (if you were in the military).

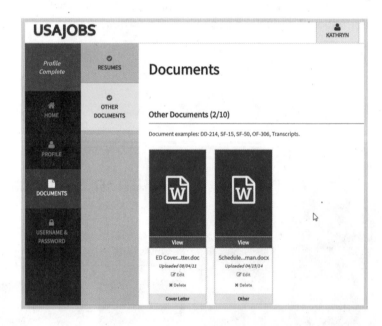

Set up your SAVED JOBS and SAVED SEARCHES and monitor your applications on your application tracking page!

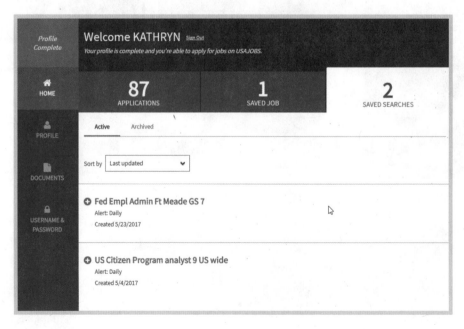

Excepted Service Federal Jobs

★ ★ ★ ★ ★

"As a spouse and a parent, my career was on the back burner, but a federal career will now allow me professional growth and advancement."

Kryptos sculpture at the CIA Headquarters building. www.cia.gov

What is the Difference Between Competitive and Excepted Service?

Federal jobs are split into two types of service. The two types of jobs can even be found at the same agency, such as at NASA.

COMPETITIVE SERVICE:
GS-2210 Information Technologist

EXCEPTED SERVICE:
Astronaut

Competitive Service:

★ Competitive Service jobs are subject to OPM's hiring rules, pay scales, etc.

★ Traditional competitive hiring process applies

★ Can earn tenure a.k.a. "status" over time

★ Status allows you some hiring benefits

★ Cannot be easily fired

★ Earn raises according to a formula of time served

★ Open jobs must be posted online

★ Must compete for the job with the general public

Excepted Service:

★ Excepted Service jobs are excepted from the requirements of the civil service laws or from competitive service by statute or regulation. These appointments are used in cases when it is not feasible to use qualification standards, competitive examinations, or competitive procedures

★ OPM places positions in the excepted service under Schedules A, B, C, or D

★ Cannot earn "status"

★ Are hired at-will, more like private industry

★ Can earn raises according to performance

★ May be hired or fired for special reasons

★ Open jobs do not have to be publicly announced and most are not posted on USAJOBS

★ Do not have to compete for your job with the general public

Part Four

Examples of
Excepted Service Positions

These positions are in the excepted service. Employment in the excepted service does not confer competitive status to apply to competitive service jobs in the federal civil service.

The position expiration date (not to exceed date) may be extended based on workload and funding availability and is not subject to regulatory time limits.

CORE Program Services Specialist

FEDERAL EMERGENCY MANAGEMENT AGENCY

Agency Contact Information

1 vacancy in the following location:

📍 Bothell, WA

Work Schedule is Full Time - Temporary - Not to exceed 2 Years

Opened Thursday 5/25/2017
(0 day(s) ago)

🕒 Closes Thursday 6/1/2017
(7 day(s) away)

Salary Range
$53,735.00 to $69,859.00 / Per Year

Series & Grade
IC-0301-09/09

Promotion Potential
09

Supervisory Status
No

Foreign Language Teacher Japanese

U.S. ARMY TRAINING AND DOCTRINE COMMAND

Agency Contact Information

Few vacancies in the following location:

📍 Monterey, CA

Work Schedule is Full Time - Temporary NTE Varies

Opened Wednesday 8/31/2016
(267 day(s) ago)

🕒 Closes Tuesday 5/30/2017
(5 day(s) away)

Salary Range
$35,009.00 to $89,805.00 / Per Year

Series & Grade
AD-1701-02/04

Supervisory Status
No

The Resume Place, Inc. | www.resume-place.com   81

Sample Job Block for Excepted Service Resume: Social Worker

SOCIAL WORK INTERN
VA Palo Alto Health Care System
Palo Alto, California
Supervisor: XXXXX; May be Contacted.

XXXX to XXXX
30 hours/week
Salary: XXXX stipend

GRADUATE FIELD PLACEMENT INTERNSHIP working in the inpatient psychiatry unit at VA Palo Alto Health Care System.

PLANNED DIRECT CLINICAL SERVICES AND TREATMENT for Veterans of diverse cultures who were diagnosed with depression, PTSD, and other affective disorders with a range of time since initial diagnosis. Provided ongoing clinical services, including one-on-one counseling and therapy with Veterans, support for families, and establishing community-based services for care beyond discharge from the inpatient setting. Assessed psychosocial functioning, conducted psychosocial assessments, short-term treatment plans, case management, and assisted in the discharge of clients.

PERFORMED INITIAL DIAGNOSTIC EVALUATIONS. Acknowledged for my skills in completing comprehensive psychosocial assessments in a thorough and goal-oriented manner. Knowledge of medical terminology and mental health diagnoses, disabilities and treatment. Implemented psychosocial treatment and performed supportive problem solving and crisis interventions and upheld procedures for Veterans in inpatient psychiatry. Assessed need for continued treatment and disposition of patients.

COMMUNICATION AND COLLABORATION. Worked extensively with Veterans, family members, informal and formal care providers, and the operators of Residential Care Facilities. Coordinated placements in facilities including skilled nursing and long-term locked facilities. Established clear communication with Veterans, family members, friends, and other professionals. Collaborated with interdisciplinary team members on a weekly basis and/or daily basis on the progress of the client and to achieve project/program goals. Participated in weekly clinical supervision and group training and consultations. Provided consultation services to primary care providers, psychiatrist, therapist and/or other staff on psychosocial needs of client.

REFERRED CASES within VA Substance Abuse Programs to other clinicians when indicated. Adept at consulting with, coordinating with, and referring to community-based service organizations (e.g., federal/state/local social services agencies). Provided community resources and made appropriate referrals to assist clients in their area of living.

KEY ACCOMPLISHMENTS:
- ∞ I was the primary clinician for an older Veteran with two suicide attempts in a short period of time. In addition to his suicidal ideation and impulse control issues, he was grappling with substance abuse and extended grief. I collaborated with the Veteran, family members, psychiatrist, and psychologist to set up a full range of psychiatric services and group therapies. I conducted extensive research on community resources and assisted him in identifying volunteer opportunities and classes. He was very interested in teaching others and I found an opportunity for him to do so at a local library. As a result of my efforts, the Veteran connected not only with the VA, but built community connections and activities for his future orientation.
- ∞ Together with another intern, I designed and taught weekly psycho-education groups grounded in evidence-based practice (EBP).

"Because we are moving every 1 to 4 years, I can continue my career at each installation. I know that the government is 'family friendly'."

Part Five

NAF Jobs

★ ★ ★ ★ ★ ★

What is an NAF Job?

NAF jobs are funded by the installation rather than through the Congressional appropriation process.

NAF employment is considered federal employment. It is, however, different from federal civil service employment because the monies used to pay the salaries of NAF employees come from a different source. NAF money is generated by activities such as Morale, Welfare, and Recreation (MWR) Programs and other activities that use NAF employees.

Sample Navy NAF Jobs

Search Results

1 2 NEXT LAST

Job Title	Installation	Location	Opening Date	Closing Date
Child & Youth Program Leader	NAS Corpus Christi	Texas	May, 12 2017	May, 25 2017
Financial Analyst, NF-1160-04	NSA Mid-South	Tennessee	May, 19 2017	May, 26 2017
Regional Program Analyst, NF-0343-04	NSA Naples	Italy	May, 12 2017	May, 26 2017
Child & Youth Program Assistant Director, NF-1702-03	NSA Mid-South	Tennessee	May, 1 2017	May, 29 2017
Child and Youth Program School Liaison Officer, NF-1701-04	NS Rota	Spain	May, 16 2017	May, 30 2017
Embedded Resiliency Counselor, NF-0101-04	NSA Bahrain	Bahrain	May, 16 2017	May, 30 2017
General Manager (Lodging), FFR17-0288	CFA Okinawa	Japan	May, 1 2017	May, 31 2017
Rec Specialist/Fitness Coordinator, NF-0188-03	NAS Corpus Christi	Texas	May, 12 2017	May, 31 2017
Regional Training & Performance Improvement Specialist, NF-1712-04	CFA Yokosuka	Japan	May, 17 2017	May, 31 2017
Housekeeping Manager, NF-1173-03	NB Coronado	California	May, 11 2017	Jun, 1 2017
Marketing Specialist, NF-1035-03	NAS Meridian	Mississippi	May, 17 2017	Jun, 1 2017
Recreation Specialist (Physical Fitness), NF-0188-03	CFA Chinhae	Korea	May, 19 2017	Jun, 2 2017
Supervisory Recreation Specialist (Indoor/Outdoor Sports), NF-0188-03	NAS Lemoore	California	May, 3 2017	Jun, 3 2017
Community Recreation Director, NF-1101-04	NAS Corpus Christi	Texas	May, 23 2017	Jun, 5 2017
Generalist Advocate Counselor, NF-0101-04	NAS Fallon	Nevada	May, 1 2017	Jun, 5 2017

Part Five

Army:
www.USAJOBS.gov
Search: "NAF Army"

Navy:
www.navymwr.org/jobs/
and USAJOBS
On USAJOBS, search: "NAF Navy"

Air Force:
www.nafjobs.org/viewjobs.aspx
On USAJOBS, search "NAF Air Force"

Marine Corps:
www.usmc-mccs.org/careers/ (click
on Prospective Employees under Job
Search & Apply)
On USAJOBS, search "NAF USMC"

NAF Employment Benefits

Who Can Receive NAF Employment Benefits?

NAF positions are classified as either "flexible" or "regular." Flexible employees have work schedules that depend on the needs of the activity. These employees may work a minimum of zero hours to a maximum of 40 hours per week, and do not receive benefits. Regular employees work between 20 and 40 hours a week depending on position requirements, and are entitled to receive benefits.

Employee Benefits Available to All Regular Full-Time and Regular Part-Time Civilian NAF Employees:

Medical and Dental
Life Insurance
Optional and Dependent Life Insurance
Accidental Death and Dismemberment
401(k) Savings Plan
Group Retirement Plan
Family Friendly Leave Program
Flexible Spending Account
Long-Term Care
Short-Term Disability
Leave (Sick & Vacation)

Benefits and Privileges

All NAF employees are encouraged to enjoy the use of NAF facilities and take advantage of a variety of employee benefits. (Facilities may vary from base to base.) Facilities include:
Exchanges
Lodging & Dining Clubs
Childcare Facilities
Movie Theaters & Parks
Swimming Pools & Fitness Centers
Golf Courses
Bowling Centers
Marinas & Ocean Fishing
Libraries
Hobby Shops
Discount Tickets to your favorite places and Leisure Travel Deals
Flexible Schedules
Training Opportunities
Tuition Assistance at applicable commands
Balance of Work & Family Life
Employee Assistance Program (EAP)
Paid Holidays
Financial Wellness Program
All of this in a secure, fast-paced, professional, family-oriented working environment.

For Employees and Retirees

The DOD implemented the Health Benefits Program (HBP) on January 1, 2000. It provides comprehensive benefits which include hospitalization, prescription drugs, medical, surgical, preventive, mental health, substance abuse, vision, and dental care.

U.S. Army MWR NAF Position Benefits: http://www.armymwr.com/naf-benefits.aspx

Writing Your NAF Resume

Use the USAJOBS and Outline Format resume samples you see in this book to create your resume to apply for an NAF position.

Air Force NAF Resume Requirements

Here is information from the Air Force about the NAF resume. They are asking for only two pages! For other branches, though, you could write more if you have more extensive experience.

LIMIT RESUME TO TWO PAGES ONLY.

NOTE: Submission of a resume certifies that to the best of your knowledge and belief, all of the information you claim is true, correct, complete and made in good faith. You understand that false or fraudulent information could result in termination of Federal employment, and may be punishable by fine or imprisonment.

Name:
Social Security Number:
Candidate source: (NAF, APF, Military or Non-Federal Applicant)
Mailing Address:
Home Phone Number:
Work Phone Number (Commercial):
Work Phone Number (DSN):
Email Address:

EXPERIENCE SUMMARY:
Describe in a few words, a summary of the skills you possess. Emphasize those skills in occupations you are interested in being considered for to include promotion, reassignment or change to lower grade (e.g., Club Manager, Lodging Manager, Golf Manager, Business Specialist).

EXPERIENCE:
Enter the following information beginning with your most recent employment
Start and End Dates (month and four-digit year)
Hours Per Week (If less than 40 hours)
Position Title, Pay Plan, Series, and Grade (if Federal civilian position, otherwise, show military rank after position title, if appropriate)
Organization name (agency or company)
Complete mailing address of organization
Supervisor's name
Supervisor's phone number

Provide a brief description of your work experience. Limit each summary to one block of experience per position held (Do not combine your entire work history into one single paragraph). If your experience describes a Federal civilian position in the same series but at different grade levels, include month and year promoted to each grade. Indicate if temporary promotion or detail. Include all major tasks. Any systems you worked with or on and specific software programs you used. Any regulations, directives, instructions etc., you have worked with, implemented, researched or developed. Any special programs you may have managed. If applicable, number of employees supervised and whether position was as 1st or 2nd level supervisor.

FORMAL EDUCATION:

List degree earned (e.g., AA, BA, MBA, etc.), major, name of college or university, year degree awarded, GPA and total semester or quarter hours earned

If your highest level of education is high school, list either the highest grade you completed, the year you graduated or the date you were awarded your GED

EDUCATIONAL COURSE WORK (OPTIONAL):

Complete the following education information ONLY IF you are documenting courses that may satisfy the minimum education requirements for the types of positions for which you are applying. List all college-level courses you completed (including those failed) that are directly related to the types of positions for which you are applying. List graduate and undergraduate courses separately. Provide information for each course within the appropriate academic field (e.g., biology, mechanical engineering, economics, and sociology). Include the descriptive title and course code, completion date, grade, number of semester, quarter or classroom hours (for education completed at business, secretarial, technical school or military schools) and graduate and undergraduate classes.

LICENSES/CERTIFICATIONS:

List professional licenses and certificates and date certified.

AWARDS:

List any honors, awards and special accomplishments achieved and dates received.

OTHER INFORMATION:

List other relevant information [Professional memberships in professional/honor societies, professional publications, language proficiencies (non-English) in which you have near-native fluency, leadership activities, public speaking, typing, or stenography proficiencies].

NAF Resume Sample

Two-page Private Industry Resume Targeting HR Assistant / Administration

Jennifer Morris

111 Altus Street / Warner Robins, GA 31088 / Cell: 333-333-3333 / Jmorris203@gmail.com

---

CAREER FOCUS: Human Resources | Payroll & Benefits Administration

PROFESSIONAL PROFILE

Recent graduate with a BA in Business Administration and hands-on experience in Human Resources administration, including recruitment, training, payroll, and benefits administration. A performance-driven achiever with exemplary organizational, time management, writing, and analytical skills. Proficient in managing accounting procedures, ensuring accurate cash transactions and recordkeeping, and meeting deadlines.

Skills Summary:
- Human Resource Management – Benefits Administration – Recruitment – Onboarding & Training
- Business Administration – Accounting – Managerial Finance – Strategic Planning
- Technical & Analytical Writing – Business Communications – Conflict Resolution – Negotiation
- SWOT Analysis – Data Collection & Statistical Analysis – Economic & Qualitative Analysis
- Microsoft Office (Word, Excel, PowerPoint), Human Resource Information Systems (HRIS)

EDUCATION

Bachelor of Arts in Business Administration, July 2016; GPA: 3.97/ 4.00 – Summa Cum Laude
Ashford University-Forbes School of Business, Clinton, IA

Graduate Level Courses in Management Communication with Technology & Organizational Behavior

Recognized for Academic Achievement with membership in the Sigma Beta Delta Honor Society, Golden Key International Honour Society & Alpha Sigma Lambda Honor Society

---

PROFESSIONAL EXPERIENCE

BROWN MACKIE COLLEGE, Albuquerque, NM   01/2010 - 10/2011
Human Resource Assistant; Records Assistant (09/2010-10/2011);
Receptionist (01/2010-09/2010)
Supervisor: John Mack (333) 333-3333

Managed staff recruitment, selection, and placement; new hire orientation and training; and records management for Brown Mackie College - Albuquerque; a for-profit college managed by the Education Management Corporation (EDMC), Pittsburgh, PA. As Receptionist, managed front desk reception, multi-line phone, correspondence, file and records management, and meeting coordination.

- Recruited and selected staff for lower-graded clerical, administrative, technical, teaching, and other professional positions. Assisted Regional HR Manager with establishing crediting plans, matching applicants to positions, and making job offers. Managed and updated vacancy announcements.

- Conducted employee onboarding and training. Provided HR guidance to staff about payroll, benefits and other HR areas. Assisted with benefits administration and special events, including student open houses.

Jennifer Morris | Page Two

- Maintained academic files for over 300 current and former students; tracked student placement and testing scores for Admissions Department; and performed managed personnel and accrediting agency files for 50+ employees using EDMC proprietary database. Prepared reports on recruitment/placement activities.

- Provided diverse administrative support to HR and the Registrar. Managed confidential student records, schedules and files. Prepared correspondence and reports, including student attendance reports.

- ✓ Achieved zero errors on personnel and accrediting files from the Accrediting Council for Independent Colleges and Schools (ACICS) inspection; contributed to zero errors on Registrar's student academic files.

- ✓ Designed new front office documents for the Admissions Department that improved sign-in of guests and logging of phone and online inquiries. Shared new documents with front office staff of newly-opened affiliated schools to assure a cohesive enrollment process. (Jan-Sept 2010).

- ✓ Trained part-time receptionists in front office duties, facilitating a seamless transition to full-time positions. (Jan-Sept 2010)

CICI'S PIZZA BUFFET, Albuquerque, NM   02/2009 - 01/2010
Certified Shift Manager

Managed high volume restaurant operations. Managed and scheduled team of 15 semi-skilled, hourly employees per shift. Oversaw daily financial management, reporting, cost control, and recordkeeping. Tracked inventory control in the Point of Sale (POS) system. Managed HR activities including staff screening, interviewing, discipline, employee relations and training/professional development. Recommended new hires to General Manager.
- ✓ Trained staff on food service operations and procedures to ensure high standards for restaurant cleanliness, food quality, safety, and guest satisfaction.

- ✓ Evaluated staff skills and performance. Recommended promotions, training, or new positions to develop staff to their fullest potential.

MCDONALDS, Albuquerque, NM   11/2007 - 02/2009
Shift Manager

Managed team of 15-20 semi-skilled, hourly part-time and full-time employees per shift in a high volume, fast-paced fast food restaurant. Managed diverse HR activities, including staff training and development, timesheet and food service log maintenance and verification. Managed general operations such as cost control, tracking of sales and labor costs, customer service, and inventory control. Ensured strict adherence with proper safety and food preparation procedures. Updated employee time sheets and food safety logs.
- ✓ Promptly resolved guest complaints, taking any and all appropriate actions to turn dissatisfied guests into return guests.

- ✓ Monitored and controlled food and labor costs by reducing waste, theft and inefficient scheduling.

- ✓ Trained and developed team members' skills for best performance.

- ✓ Strategically used the Point of Sale (POS) system to track and manage customer wait times and improve employee performance.

- ✓ Meticulously maintained registers by skimming drawers hourly. This practice deterred and minimized internal and external theft.

Derived Preference for Military Spouses

★ ★ ★ ★ ★ ★

"When my spouse retires, and transitions out, federal employment will provide me with steady employment and income for our household while my spouse begins a new job search."

What is Derived Preference?

Derived Preference is a method by which you, as the spouse, widow/widower, or mother of a veteran may be eligible to claim veterans' preference when your veteran is unable to use it. You will be given XP Preference (10 points) in appointment if you meet the eligibility criteria.

Both a mother and a spouse (including widow or widower) may be entitled to preference on the basis of the same veteran's service if they both meet the requirements. However, neither may receive preference if the veteran is living and is qualified for federal employment.

Spouses are eligible when your veteran has a service-connected disability and has been unable to qualify for any position in the civil service.

Widows/Widowers are eligible if you did not divorce your veteran spouse, have not remarried, or the remarriage was annulled, and the veteran:

★ served during a war or during the period April 28, 1952, through July 1, 1955, or in a campaign or expedition for which a campaign medal has been authorized; OR

★ died while on active duty that included service described immediately above under conditions that would not have been the basis for other than an honorable or general discharge.

Mothers of deceased veterans are eligible when your son or daughter died under honorable conditions while on active duty during a war or in a campaign or expedition for which a campaign medal has been authorized. Additionally, you must:

★ be or have been married to the father of your veteran; AND

★ live with a permanently disabled husband; OR

★ be widowed, divorced, or separated from the veteran's father and have not remarried; OR

★ if remarried be widowed, divorced, or legally separated from your husband at the time you claim derived preference.

Mothers of disabled veterans are eligible if your son or daughter was separated with an honorable or general discharge from active duty, including training service in the Reserves or National Guard, and is permanently and totally disabled from a service-connected injury or illness. Additionally, you must:

★ be or have been married to the father of your veteran; AND

★ live with a permanently disabled husband; OR

★ be widowed, divorced, or separated from the veteran's father and have not remarried; OR

★ if remarried, be widowed, divorced, or legally separated from your husband at the time you claim derived preference.

Source: https://www.fedshirevets.gov/job/familypref/index.aspx

Successful Application with Derived Preference: Results Email from DOD

---------- Forwarded message ----------
From: **Vacancy ID: 1734946** <<u>usastaffingoffice@opm.gov</u>>
Date: Mon, Aug 8, 2016 at 3:26 PM
Subject: Notification Letter Vacancy ID: 1734946
TO: <u>susanne</u>

DOJ - HEADQUARTERS COMPONENTS
JUSTICE MANAGEMENT DIVISION
145 N STREET NE SUITE 9W 300
WASHINGTON DC 20530

Dear SUSANNE

This refers to the application you recently submitted to this office for the position below:

Position Title: Administrative Specialist
Promotion Potential: 09
Vacancy ID: 1734946
Agency: Offices, Boards and Divisions
Considered For: COMMUNITY RELATIONS SERVICES
Duty Location: Washington DC, DC

We have reviewed your application and found you qualified for the position listed above. *Your name has been referred to the employing agency for consideration.*

Part Six

After Resume: Derived Preference

USAJOBS Federal Resume Targeting Admin, Database, Tracking, Computers, Customer Svcs

SUSANNE MILTON

1012 Alexander Way

Alexandria, VA 22309 US

(703) 444-4444

Desired locations:

United States - VA – Alexandria United States - VA - Fort Belvoir Germany -Germersheim
Germany - Stuttgart

Work Experience:

AFBA Armed Forces Benefit Association

909 N Washington Street

Alexandria, VA   22314 United States

09/2009 - Present

Salary: 60,000.00 USD Per Year

Hours per week: 40

New Business Analyst

Duties, Accomplishments and Related Skills:

PROCESS APPLICATIONS for insurance policies with a total value between $80-$200 million per month,
following strict underwriting guidelines and ensuring federal and state regulations and laws are properly
followed. Analyze applications and forward to medical underwriters when necessary. Update and verify
customer information in LifePro and AS400 databases.

COMMUNICATE IN WRITTEN AND ORAL FORM to customers and staff to obtain additional information
regarding over 1,000 new applications monthly. Provide updates of status to staff and inform leadership
of issues requiring attention. Review and acknowledge beneficiary change forms and other legal
documents submitted by customers ensuring policies, regulations and laws are adhered to. Provide
feedback to management regarding system problems and trends.

DELIVER OUTSTANDING CUSTOMER SERVICE by notifying 50-100 customers per month facing decrease in coverage via mail. Communicate with customers via phone and mail, providing customers with information on changes and options resulting in upgrades of coverage in 50-80% of policies.

TRACK, MAINTAIN AND ANALYZE DATA on customer lapsed policies utilizing Microsoft Excel spreadsheet, analyzing for determination of reinstatement or termination resulting in reinstatement of up to 60% of accounts. Report required actions, based on analysis, to the accounting department for resolution.

* Preserve long-time customers by manually maintaining and tracking a detailed spreadsheet of older policies and making adjustments of workflows in Salesforce and coordination through LifePro.

WRITE, EDIT AND PREPARE REPORTS AND CORRESPONDENCE relating to policies, beneficiaries, application status, and workflows. Prepare reports utilizing Salesforce Customer Relation Management System (CRS), LifePro and AS400.

KEY ACCOMPLISHMENTS:

* Report suspicious trends of insurance agents to VP of Operations and help find solutions for better communication and optimum productivity.

* Work on special projects to support conversion of member files and policies to new administrative system.

* Propose new procedures to ensure maximum productivity in the New Business department. Improvements I suggested to increase productivity:

1. Suggested giving people an additional computer monitor (to process each case we use multiple screens for AS400, sometimes ID3, Salesforce, Life Pro and Image besides Accurint and Lotus Notes for e-mails). Time saved: between 2-5 minutes per case. This means we can process 50 cases and save 1-2 hours; we can easily process 10-20 more cases per day.

2. Suggested creating specific queues to target certain actions to avoid unnecessary volume increase and delay of cases that are ready to be approved. Those 'special action' cases were sent to people's personal queues or pended by people who did not know what to do—and therefore were neglected. Instead of being pended in the general queue it would go to the 'Rate queue', for example, if a different rate was offered (i.e., status or graded instead of preferred due to medical history). Time saved: per day there might be 5-10 cases in that queue.

3. Suggested implementing certain 'product-specific' workflows in Salesforce. For example, the Final

Expense plan is age specific and low coverage—if the workflow is for this product only, it can be actioned by the employees who process this product and are more familiar with its specific processing rules. Time saved: 2-5 minutes per case, with up to 10 cases per day.

4. Created a spreadsheet for Medical Reject records found while processing for the medical Underwriters to utilize in reviewing cases before they are being sent to our external underwriter. This helps a daily review of problem cases by Medical Underwriters instead of waiting in a medical queue with other cases/ issues to review. It will prevent us to jet-issue before thoroughly checking – therefore it saves us time and trouble later on when we receive a claim and have to go out for medical info from the hospital or doctor office to ask for medical history. Time saved: up to 1 hour per day.

5. Asked for access to perform certain system functions myself instead of having to ask team leader or Medical Underwriter (and then wait for them to read my e-mail and respond/ action the request, which sometimes took a day up to a week). Examples: moving incorrectly assigned cases from restricted queues, removing errors in Life Pro system, changing document type in Image, merging incorrect records (Social Security numbers).

6. Asked for automated generation of Beneficiary Change Forms with letter request (top portion) already pre-filled with name and policy type to save time and avoid human error. Time saved: 2-3 minutes per letter, approximately 50 letters per day.

7. Suggested a simpler, better welcome package. Soon there will be a booklet printed/collated.

Supervisor: John Patron (555-444-3333)

Okay to contact this Supervisor: Yes

AFBA Armed Forces Benefit Association

909 N Washington Street

Alexandria, VA   22314 United States

05/2002 - 09/2009

Salary: 45,000.00 USD Per Year

Hours per week: 40

Sr. Marketing Support Administrator

Duties, Accomplishments and Related Skills:

HUMAN RESOURCES LIAISON: Worked closely with the Human Resources Department to provide finished documents for position evaluations, job descriptions, and position vacancies. Provided detailed information regarding position requirements and eligibility to apply to potential candidates.

TEAM LEADER: Interviewed and selected Console Operator and Administrative Assistants. Reviewed work performance and gave orientation for new hires. Supervised and provided ongoing training to five employees while coordinating daily work requirements, as well as performing any necessary tasks to meet the daily completion deadlines

SUPPLIES AND INVENTORY MANAGEMENT: Monitored and organized stockroom; ordered office supplies weekly; reviewed inventory levels. Advised management on inventory and supplies required; advised staff members on availability of inventory. Organized and filed reports, updated meeting and reminder calendars on Lotus Notes, and prepared packages for mailing via USPS, FedEx, and UPS.

COMPUTER SKILLS: Lotus Notes, Word, Calendar Management, Excel.

ADMINISTRATIVE: Provided a high level of support to Operations Department along with Senior Vice President of Operations and other executive staff. Translated German documents and called doctor's offices in Germany for Claims and Medical Underwriting departments. Attended weekly supervisory meetings with Senior Vice President of Operations to guarantee highest level of productivity from the department and to ensure that production was in accordance with daily reports. Maintained confidential records, screened e-mails and phone calls, and coordinated departmental calendar on Lotus Notes. Monitored/performed quality control on daily mail output and notified IT department and supervisor of any discrepancies and problems requiring resolution.

Before Resume: Derived Preference

One Job Block, Popular Bullet Format, Not Targeted Toward Any Position

SUSANNE MILTON

Professional Experience:

Armed Forces Benefit Association (AFBA), Alexandria, VA 22314
(7/99 – Present):

New Business and Beneficiary Analyst
09/10 – Present

+ Process membership applications, issue or decline new life insurance policies while following strict underwriting guidelines
+ Assess applicant insurability and request pertinent additional information from clients and agents
+ Analyze weekly spreadsheet 'Terminated/ lapsed member accounts with money in suspense' –   reinstate policies if applicable and report to Accounting department the cases from which a refund should be issued
+ Run monthly report 'Lock-In Age up' for Group Term Life Insurance product. Create workflows and update member accounts on Life Pro accordingly to assure correct Lock-In adjustments are made manually on anniversary date
+ Respond to action worksheets and other requests related to application issues
+ Review and acknowledge Beneficiary Change Forms as well as other legal documents submitted by members
+ Provide feedback to management regarding system problems or any related trends
+ Generate, review and mail any necessary correspondence related to an application

- Review and process requests for replacement and change of coverage amounts.
- Assist the Underwriting Department with the processing of life insurance applications, while following strict underwriting guidelines
- Work on special projects to support conversion of member files and policies to new administrative system
- Research reasons for lapsed member accounts with funds - report to Accounting department which accounts can be re-activated/ or terminated with refund of money in suspense.
- Compose letters to applicants in order to clarify questions or request information   needed to complete application process.
- Provide clerical support to ensure efficient office operations and use software application programs for word processing and database management to support office activities.
- Type a variety of documents in draft or final form and review them for correct spelling, punctuation, grammar, format and style.
- Propose new procedures to ensure maximum productivity in the New Business department.
- Report suspicious trends of insurance agents to VP of Operations and help find solutions for better communication and optimum productivity.

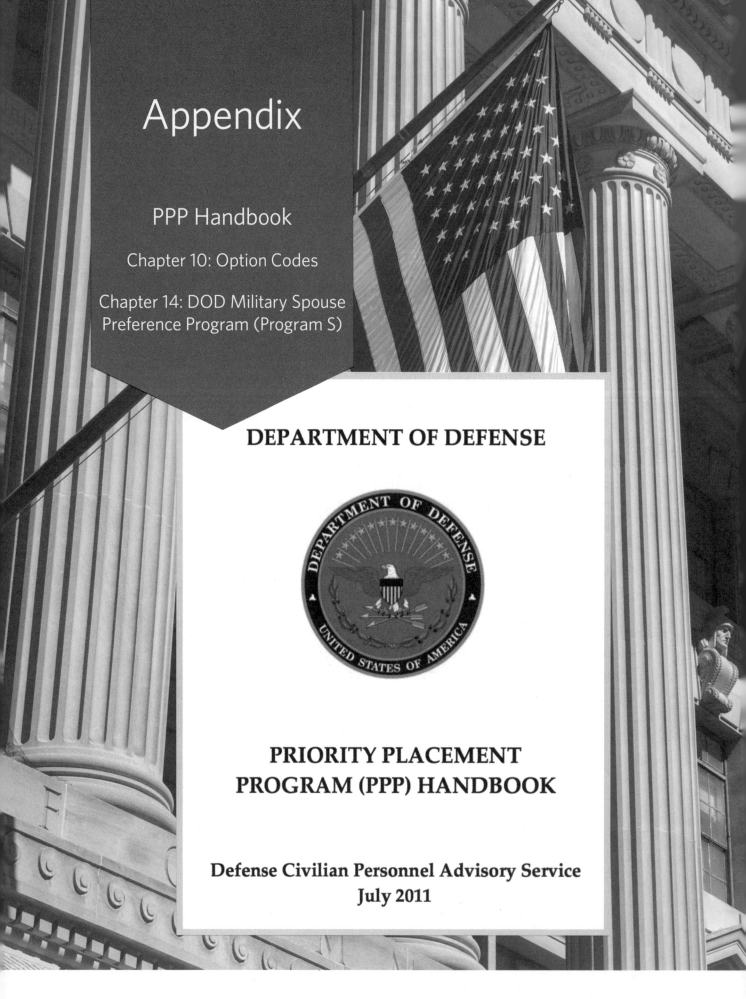

Appendix

PPP Handbook

Chapter 10: Option Codes

Chapter 14: DOD Military Spouse
Preference Program (Program S)

DEPARTMENT OF DEFENSE

**PRIORITY PLACEMENT
PROGRAM (PPP) HANDBOOK**

Defense Civilian Personnel Advisory Service
July 2011

CHAPTER 10

OPTION CODES

TABLE OF CONTENTS

SECTIONS   **Page**

    A. Purpose   10-1
    B. Procedural Requirements   10-1

APPENDICES

    A. Option Codes   10-A-1

CHAPTER 10

OPTION CODES

A. PURPOSE

The purpose of this Chapter is to explain the proper use of option codes, which are used in registration to more specifically define qualifications and in requisitioning to clarify job requirements.

B. PROCEDURAL REQUIREMENTS

Except for the six generic options (see B.6., below) and the NOA option code (see B.2. below), option codes may be used only with the specific occupational series under which they are listed in Appendix A.

1. The registration format will accommodate up to 10 option codes per skill line. Decisions as to which options, if any, may be used, are based solely on a registrant's qualifications. An option code should never be entered more than once for the same occupational series.

2. NOA, which equates to "No Option Applicable," may only be used when the registrant has experience in a particular series that does not correspond to an existing option code, and it may be used in combination with other option codes. NOA is never appropriate when all of the registrant's experience in a given series can be categorized with some other option code(s).

a. **Example 1**. A GS-501 employee currently specializes in civilian pay, and this work corresponds to option code CVY. She previously held a GS-501 position in the travel pay section, and this experience can be reflected with option code TPY. In between these two jobs, she performed GS-501 duties that do not correspond to any of the available option codes in Appendix A. Base on these three assignments, the employee can register with option codes CVY, TPY and NOA.

b. **Example 2**. A GS-501 co-worker of the employee in Example 1 currently specializes in civilian pay (CVY) and in a prior assignment worked exclusively with military pay (MPY). He has no other GS-501 experience. The employee can register with option codes CVY and MPY, but is not eligible to register with NOA.

3. The requisition format will accommodate up to 3 option codes. If a position legitimately requires more than 3 option codes, the HRO must use the 3 that are most essential to the position. NOA must be used when there are no applicable option codes in Appendix A, and it cannot be used in combination with any other option codes.

4. Normally, requisitions submitted with NOA will not match registrations unless the corresponding skill line includes NOA. The only exceptions are DAT (Data Transcription), OAA (Office Automation), STC (Stenography), FLP (Foreign Language Proficiency), or IST (Scientific & Technical Intelligence Production). When registered with these generic option codes, registrants will match positions in the same series that are requisitioned with NOA.

5. If registered with two or more options, registrants will match requisitions submitted with one or both of the options. If registered with three or more options, registrants will match requisitions submitted with one, two, or all three of the options.

6. An option code should not be used when it does nothing more than duplicate the series title (e.g., ELD (Electronics)) should not be used with the GS-855, Electronic Engineer, series).

7. DAT, OAA, STC and FLP may be used with any appropriate GS series, except as prohibited by B.5. above. IST may be used with multiple series, but positions requiring this option are normally limited to the GS-132 series and the GS-400, 800, 1300, and 1500 occupational groups. Unless identified in Appendix A of this Chapter, not counting the preceding generic option codes, the use of other option codes for GS-04 and below positions is inappropriate. TRA (Trainee) may be used with any pay plan except WT and with any appropriate series to identify registrants/positions in formal training programs as defined in Chapter 1, Section D. Registrants who are assigned to formal training program positions must register using the TRA option but may also register without the TRA option for the same or other appropriate series.

8. For registration and file maintenance, OAA and STC may be entered on the same skill line except as prohibited by B.5. above.

9. For registration and requisitioning purposes, either OAA or STC must be used with the GS-318 series.

➡️ 10. **GS-800 Job Family**

a. **General Engineer, GS-801 positions**. The GS-801 series normally must have at least two option codes, but a single option may be appropriate when using TRA or one of the authorized commodity options. If more than three options codes are necessary, use the three that are most essential to the position as explained in B.3. above.

b. **Commodity Options**. Commodity options codes are unique to the GS-800 job family, and unlike other options codes, they describe the environment in which the work is performed rather than the occupation skills required to perform the work. These codes do not correspond with traditional engineering disciplines, nor would they necessarily be included in specific job titles or parentheticals. When used properly, a commodity option code indicates that the duties of the position cannot be performed successfully unless the incumbent has applied his or her engineering or engineering technical skills in that particular work environment. Commodity options may be used in conjunction with other option codes.

11. **Special Procedures for 301 and 303 Series.** In order to register for positions in the 301 series with the NOA (no option applicable) option code, registrants must have previously held a position in the 301 series. The same restriction applies to 303 positions at grades GS-5 and above. Registrants who have never held a 301 or 303 position may register for either series if they are otherwise eligible and well qualified for one or more of the corresponding option codes (i.e., other than NOA) listed in this Chapter. For example, an employee whose experience has been entirely in the 560, Budget Analyst series, could register for 301 positions with the BUD (Budget) option code.

12. To better understand the relationship between options codes and their respective series, refer to applicable classification and qualifications standards. Recommendations to alter, add, or delete the option codes contained in Appendix A may be referred for consideration through DoD Component channels to PPSB.

CHAPTER 10

APPENDIX A

OPTION CODES

Series	Series Title	Option Code	Option Title
	Any Appropriate Series	NOA	No Option Applicable
	Any Appropriate GS Series	DAT	Data Transcription
	(see Chapter 10, Section B.6.)	OAA	Office Automation
		STC	Stenography
		TRA	Trainee
		FLP+	Foreign Language Proficiency
		IST	Scientific & Technical Intelligence Production
	Any Appropriate WG Series	TRA	Trainee
018	Safety & Occupational Health	ORB	Ordnance
		MDC	Medical
080	Security Administration	FOC	Foreign Ownership, Control & Influence
		INA	Industrial
		INB	Automation
		IND	Disclosure
		INF	Information Security/ Classification Management
		INO	Operations Security
		INS	Information Systems
		INT	Technical
		PEB	Personnel
		PHB	Physical
081	Fire Protection and Prevention (GS-05 and above only)	AIG	Airfield
		EMT	Emergency Medical Technician
		FIC	Fire Inspection
		HAZ	Hazardous Materials
		PAR	Paramedic

081	(cont'd)	STE	Structural
086	Security Assistant (GS-05 and above only)	SPF	Support Police Force
101	Social Service	ADC	Alcohol & Drug Control Officer
		EAP	Employee Assistance Program Coordinator
		EFM	Exceptional Family Member Program
		FAP	Family Advocacy Program
		FSP	Family Support Services
180	Psychology	CLI	Clinical
		PIO	Industrial/Organizational Psychology
		RES	Research
185	Social Worker	ADV	Family Advocacy
		SAB	Substance Abuse
188	Recreation Specialist	ARB	Arts
		CIN	Institutional
		COD	Community Activities
		SEB	Service Club Activities
		SPB	Sports
		YOA	Youth Activities
201 & 203	Human Resources Management/Assistance (GS-05 and above only)	HRO	Human Resources Officer/Director, Assistant Human Resources Officer/Director (GS-201 REQUISITIONS ONLY, cannot be used with any other option code)
		BEN	Employee Benefits
		CLA	Classification
		CMP	Compensation (GS-201 ONLY)
		EMC	Employee Relations
		HRD	Human Resources Development
		INS	Information Systems

201 & 203	(con't)	LBR	Labor Relations
		MIL	Military
		MOB	Mobilization (GS-201 ONLY)
		NAF	Non-Appropriated Funds (GS-201 ONLY)
		OCA	Occupational Analysis (GS-201 ONLY)
		PFM	Performance Management
		STF	Staffing
		SWA	Salary & Wage Administration (GS-201 ONLY)
		WFS	Workforce Shaping (GS-201 ONLY)
301 & 303	Misc Admin and Program Management, Misc Clerk and Assistant (GS-05 and above only)	AIM	Aircraft Maintenance and Operations
		ANA	Analysis and Planning
		BUD	Budget
		CAT	Community Activities
		CLB	Club Management
		CBD	Combat Development
		CDC	Child Development Clerk (GS-303 ONLY)
		COF	Configuration
		COR	Communications
		DPC	Drug Program Coordinator
		DRR	Disaster Response & Recovery (GS-301 Only)
		EMS	Emergency Management Specialist
		FAC	Facilities
		FIB	Financial Management
		FOA	Food Service
		FOI	Freedom of Information Act/ Public Affairs (GS-301 ONLY)
		FOP	Flight Operations
		FOR	Force Structure
		FMS	Foreign Military Sales

301& 303	(con't)	FSP	Family Support Services
		FUL	Fuels/Energy
		HCA	Health Care
		HOA	Housing
		INS	Information Systems Management
		ITN	International Affairs
		LOA	Logistics
		MED	Medical
		MLP	Military Planning/Training
		MOA	Mortuary Affairs
		MOB	Mobilization
		MPS	Missile Propulsion Systems
		MWR	Morale, Welfare, and Recreation Programs GS-301 ONLY)
		OMM	Open Mess Manager
		ORB	Ordnance
		PER	Personnel/Manpower Admin.
		PRC	Procurement
		PRO	Protocol
		PUA	Publications
		REC	Reports/Forms/Files
		REK	Recreation Services
		RMA	Resource Management
		ROA	Range Operations
		SUB	Supply
		SVC	Contract Services
		TRB	Training-Education
		YOA	Youth Activities
318	Secretary	OAA	Office Automation
		STC	Stenography
340	Program Management	ACQ	Systems Acquisition
		FMS	Foreign Military Sales
		MWR	Morale, Welfare, & Recreation Programs
		PHR	Personnel
343	Management and Program Analyst	ACQ	Systems Acquisition

343	(con't)	COZ	Cost Analyst
		FMS	Foreign Military Sales
		HCA	Health Care
		IMG	Information Management Specialist
		MAL	Manpower
		MBR	Manpower/Budget (Resource) Management
		MOB	Mobilization
		PHR	Personnel
		REC	Reports/Forms/Files
		ORB	Ordnance
		ORG	Organization and Mission
		STI	Statistical Analysis
		STP	Strategic Planning
		TEV	Test & Evaluation
		WCF	Working Capital Fund
344	Management Clerical and Assistance (GS-05 and above only)	MAL	Manpower
		REC	Reports/Forms/Files
		WOC	Work Measurement
		SPR	Systems Programmer
		MBR	Manpower/Budget (Resources) Management
346	Logistics Management (GS-12 and above only)	ACQ	Systems Acquisition
		ALS	Automation of Logistics Systems
		AIB	Aircraft
		FAC	Facilities
		FMS	Foreign Military Sales
		AUD	Automotive
		CEL	Communications-Electronics
		ILS	Integrated Logistics
		MEL	Medical Logistics
		MIB	Missile
		MNT	Maintenance
		MOB	Mobilization
		NUA	Nuclear
		ORB	Ordnance
		SHB	Ships

391	Telecommunications Specialist	ANT	Antenna
		DWT	Data Networks
		MSG	Message
		RDO	Radios
		TCN	Tech Control
		TEL	Telephones/Voice
		VVD	Voice/Video/Data
392	General Communications (GS-05 and above only)	EQD	Equipment Operation
401	General Biological Science	ENV	Environmental
		REG	Regulatory
		RMO	Range Land Management
		RSH	Research
		WLD	Wildlife
408	Ecology	REG	Regulatory
501	Financial Administration & Programs	COQ	Cost Analyst
		CPY	Contractor Payments
		CVY	Civilian Pay
		FSY	Financial System
		MPY	Military Pay
		NAF	Non-Appropriated Funds
		TPY	Travel Pay
503	Financial Clerk & Technician (GS-05 and above only)	DIS	Disbursing
		MDA	Medical
510	Accounting	ADT	Auditing
		COQ	Cost
		INE	Internal
		OPB	Operating
		SYA	Systems
		WCF	Working Capital Funds
511	Auditor	COK	Contract
		FIN	Financial
		INE	Internal
560	Budget Analyst	WCF	Working Capital Funds
		WSP	Acquisition of Weapons/ Support Systems

601	General Health Sciences	CGT	Cytogenetic Technologist
		CYT	Cytotechnologist
		EXP	Exercise Specialist
		HPM	Health Promotion Manager
		NEC	Necropsy
602	Medical Officer	ADM	Administration
		ANE	Anesthesiology
		DER	Dermatology
		EME	Emergency Medicine
		FAM	Family Practice
		GPR	General Practice
		GER	Geriatrics
		IMN	Internal Medicine
		NUR	Neurology
		OBG	OB/GYN
		OCH	Occupational Health
		OPH	Ophthalmology
		OTH	Orthopedics
		PAT	Pathology
		PDS	Pediatrics
		PSY	Psychiatry
		PUH	Public Health
		RAD	Radiology
		SRG	Surgery
		URO	Urology
610	Nursing (GS-08 and above only)	ADM	Administration
		AMB	Ambulatory
		ANE	Nurse Anesthetist
		CLI	Clinical Nurse
		CHN	Community Health Nurse
		CNC	Nurse Consultant
		CNM	Nurse Midwife
		CNS	Nurse Specialist
		CRI	Critical Care
		DIB	Diabetes
		EDU	Nurse Educator
		EMR	Emergency Room
		LND	Labor & Delivery
		MSG	Medical-Surgical
		NEO	Neonatal
		NFA	First Assistant

610	(con't)	NIC	Neonatal Intensive Care
		OBG	OB/GYN
		OCH	Occupational Health
		ONC	Oncology
		OPR	Operating Room
		NPR	Nurse Practitioner
		PDS	Pediatrics
		PSY	Psychiatric Nurse
		RES	Research
		SCB	Cardiac
640	Health Aid & Technician (GS-05 and above only)	DER	Dermatology
		EMT	Emergency Medical Tech
		HTI	Industrial Hygiene
		HTA	Audiology
		HTC	Cardiovascular
		HTM	Mental Health
		HTO	Optometry
		HTP	Physical Therapy
		NUT	Nutrition
		OTL	Otolaryngology
		PAR	Paramedic
		URO	Urology
644	Medical Technologist	MTC	Chemistry
		MTH	Hematology
		MTM	Microbiology
647	Diagnostic Radiological Technologist (GS-05 and above only)	CTI	Comp. Tomography Imaging
		MAM	Mammography
671	Health Systems Specialist	CTR	Contract Administration
		HCA	Health Care
		RSK	Risk Management/Patient Safety/Compliance
680	Dentist	PRS	Prosthodontist
		PED	Periodontics
800	The following Professional Engineering and Engineering Technician Series: 801, 802, 806, 810, 818, 819, 830, 840, 850, 854, 855, 856, 861, 871, 893, 896	AAB	Navigation Systems

800	(con't)		ACA	Acoustics
			ACQ	Systems Acquisition
			ACS	Aircraft Systems
			AEC	Aerospace
			ARA	Architecture
			AUD	Automotive
			CAL	Calibration
			CCC	Command, Control, Communications & Computers
			CHA	Chemical
			CHD*	Computer Hardware
			CIB	Civil
			CTL	Coastal
			COH	Construction
			COJ	Cost Estimating
			COR	Communications
			COS	Contracts
			CST*	Computer Software
			CWO	Civil Works Oper and Maint
			CWP	Civil Works Planning
			DEB	Design
			DEV	Development
			ELA	Electrical
			ELD	Electronics
			ELF	Electronic Warfare
			ENV	Environmental
			FAC	Facilities
			GEO	Geotechnical
			HVC	Heating, Ventilation & Air Conditioning
			HYD	Hydraulic
			HYP	Hydropower
			HZW	Hazardous Waste
			INA	Industrial
			INC*	Instrumentation
			LAB	Laser
			MAH	Materials
			MAS	Machinery Systems
			MEA	Mechanical
			MIB*	Missile
			NAV	Naval
			NUA	Nuclear
			ORB*	Ordnance

800	(con't)	PET	Petroleum
		PUL	Propulsion
		RDR	Radar
		REG	Regulatory
		RES	Research
		SCM	Satellite Communications
		SHB*	Ships
		SIM	Simulation
		STE	Structural
		TCS	Tactical Communications Software
		TEV	Test and Evaluation
		TRS	Training Systems
		UTA	Utilities
		WAB*	Water Resources Development
1083	Technical Writing and Editing	AIB	Aircraft
		DAC	Data Automation
		ELD	Electronics
		LOA	Logistics
		ORB	Ordnance
1101	General Business and Industry	ACQ	Systems Acquisition
		CIR	Contract Industrial Relations
		CLB	Club Management
		MKT	Marketing Programs
		MTP	Military Programs
		OMM	Open Mess Manager
		PTM	Production Management
		QAS	Quality Assurance
		REK	Recreation Services
		RPM	Real Property Management
		WCF	Working Capital Fund
1102	Contract and Procurement	ACQ	Systems Acquisition
		COL	Contract Administrator
		CON	Contract Negotiator
		COO	Contract Specialist
		COP	Contract Termination Spec.
		PRD	Price Analyst
		PRG	Procurement Administrator
		PRH	Procurement Analyst (Staff)
		PRI	Proc. Analyst (Small Business)

1150 & 1152	Industrial Specialist, Production Control	AIB	Aircraft
		AUT	Automotive (GS-1152 ONLY)
		COH	Construction (" " ")
		ELA	Electrical
		ELD	Electronics
		MAI	Materials Handling
		MEA	Mechanical
		MIB	Missile
		ORB	Ordnance
		PUL	Propulsion Systems (GS-1150 ONLY)
		SHB	Ships
1301	General Physical Science	ACA	Acoustics
1310	Physics	ACA	Acoustics
		EOP	Electro-Optics
		IOA	Ion-implantation
		LAB	Laser
		NUA	Nuclear
		OPE	Optical
		SOF	Solid State Electronics
		SYC	Systems Analysis
		THE	Thermal Physics
1320	Chemist	RES	Research
1360	Oceanography	ACA	Acoustics
1410	Librarian	ENG.	Engineering
		LAW	Legal
		MED	Medical
		PHS	Physical Science
1550	Computer Science	COR	Communications
		DEB	Design
		NET	Network
		STY	Security
1601	Facilities and Equipment	ELI	Electrical Inspection
1603	Equip, Facilities, Services Assistant (GS-05 and above only)	CEM	Cemetery

1603	(cont'd)	FAC	Facility
		PTG	Printing
		LAU	Laundry
		FOA	Food
		EFS	Equip, Facilities, Services
1670	Equipment Specialist	AIB	Aircraft
		AIF	Aircraft Propulsion Equipment
		AIH	Airframe
		AUD	Automotive
		COR	Communications
		ELA	Electrical
		ELD	Electronics
		MAB	Machinery
		MAC	Machine Tools
		MAG	Marine
		MAI	Materials Handling
		MIE	Missile Electronics
		NUA	Nuclear
		ORB	Ordnance
		SHB	Ships
17XX	General Education and Training (GS-1701, 1702, 1710, 1750) (GS-05 and above only)	CDS	Child Development
		EDS	Education Services
		GUC	Guidance Counselor
		TDD	Training Design and Development
		TEA	Training Program Effectiveness Analysis
		TEM	Tests and Measurements
		YOA	Youth Activities
1712	Instruction	AIB	Aircraft
		ATC	Air Traffic Control
		AUD	Automotive
		CBE	Combat Engineer
		CSI	Computer Science
		ELR	Electrical & Refrigeration
		ELD	Electronics
		FAE	Field Artillery
		FCS	Fire Control Systems

1712	(con't)	FLE	Flight Simulator
		HEB	Health Services
		HME	Heavy Mobile Equipment Mechanics
		LOA	Logistics
		MAG	Marine
		MIP	Military Police/Security Forces
		MIT	Military Training Administration
		NBC	Nuclear, Biological, Radiological, Chemical
		NWI	Nuclear Weapons
		ORB	Ordnance
		PGE	Power Generating Equipment (Field)
		SEC	Security
		TGI	Target Interdiction
		WPN	Weapons
18xx	Investigation	ACQ	Acquisition Systems
		CCI	Computer Crime
		ICI	Counterintelligence
		PLH	Polygraph Examiner
1910	Quality Assurance	AEC	Aerospace
		AIB	Aircraft
		AMA	Ammunition
		AUD	Automotive
		CHA	Chemical
		CLG	Clothing
		COH	Construction
		CST	Computer Software
		ELA	Electrical
		ELD	Electronics
		MAH	Materials
		MEA	Mechanical
		NUA	Nuclear
		PRE	Process
		SHA	Shipbuilding
		SUA	Subsistence
2001	Supply Specialist	ORB	Ordnance

2003	Supply Program Management	FMS	Foreign Military Sales
		ORB	Ordnance
2005	Supply Clerical & Technician (GS-05 and above only)	AMO	Ammunition
		MED	Medical
2010	Inventory Management Specialist	ORB	Ordnance
2150	Transportation Operations	AFM	Airfield Manager
		MCO	Marine Cargo Operations
		MFP	Maritime Force Protection/Anti-terrorism
		MTO	Marine Transportation Operations
		PSE	Physical Security
		SHB	Ships
2152	Air Traffic Control	STA	Station
		TOW	Terminal
		TWR	Radar Approach Control
2181	Aircraft Operations	FID	Fixed Wing
		FLB	Flight Instructor
		FLD	Flight Test Pilot
		HEA	Helicopter
		PIA	Pilot
2210	Information Technology Management	ASW	Application Software
		CSP	Customer Support
		DMT	Data Management
		EAR	Enterprise Architecture
		INX	Internet
		NET	Network Services
		OSY	Operating Systems
		STY	Security
		SYA	Systems Administrator
		SYC	Systems Analysis
4749	Maintenance Mechanic/Worker (except for TRA, the use of only one option code is not allowed)	CRP	Carpentry
		COH	Construction
		HVC	Heating, Ventilation, AC

4749	(con't)	ELA	Electrical
		ELD	Electronics
		MSN	Masonry
		PNT	Painting
		PLM	Plumbing
		SHM	Sheet Metal Fabrication
		UTA	Utilities

Defense Civilian Intelligence Personnel System (DCIPS) Option Codes			
Series	Series Title	Option Code	Option Title
	Any Appropriate Series	ING	Intelligence
		IST	Scientific and Technician Intelligence Production
080	Security Administration	INB	Automation
		IND	Disclosure
		INI	Industrial
		IIN	Information
		INO	Operations Security
		IPE	Personnel
		IPH	Physical
		INT	Technical
132	Intelligence Specialist	COA	Collection Analysis
		COM	Communications Security
		FME	Foreign Military Exploitation
		IPR	Intelligence Production
		IOP	Intelligence Operations
		ICD	Intelligence Combat Developments
		ITH	Intelligence and Threat Support
		ICI	Counterintelligence (CI)
		IAC	Acoustics Intelligence (ACINT)
		ICO	Communications Intelligence (COMINT)
		IEL	Electronic Intelligence (ELINT)
		IHU	Human Intelligence (HUMINT)
		IMI	Imagery Intelligence (IMINT)
		IMS	Measurement and Signature Intelligence (MASINT)

132	(cont'd)		IRA	Radar Intelligence (RADINT)
			ISI	Signals Intelligence (SIGINT)
			POL	Political/Military
			SCT	Scientific and Technology
			TEC	Technology Transfer

* Commodity Options

+ For registration purposes, enter language proficiency in the "Employee Information/Special Qualifications" Data Element of the registration format. (NOTE: The gaining activity determines qualifications for language proficiency after referral.)

CHAPTER 14

DoD MILITARY SPOUSE PREFERENCE PROGRAM (PROGRAM S)

TABLE OF CONTENTS

SECTIONS		Page
A.	Purpose	14-1
B.	Applicability	14-1
C.	Registration Eligibility	14-3
D.	Registration Options	14-5
E.	Registering Activity Procedures	14-6
F.	Gaining Activity Procedures	14-7
G.	Component Exceptions	14-10

APPENDIX

A.	Military Spouse Preference Program (Program S) Registration/Counseling Checklist	14-A-1

CHAPTER 14

DoD MILITARY SPOUSE PREFERENCE PROGRAM (PROGRAM S)

References: (a) Title 10, United States Code, section 1784, Employment Opportunities For Military Spouses

(b) DoD Instruction 1400.25, "DoD Civilian Personnel Management System"

(c) Title 5, Code of Federal Regulations

A. PURPOSE

The purpose of this Chapter is to prescribe registration, referral, and placement procedures for the DoD Military Spouse Preference Program (Program S). Authority for this program is provided by reference (a) as implemented by Volume 315 of reference (b). All Program A procedures apply except as modified in this Chapter.

B. APPLICABILITY

1. This Chapter applies to spouses of active duty military members of the U.S. Armed Forces, including the U.S. Coast Guard and full-time National Guard or Reserves, who desire priority consideration for competitive service positions at DoD activities in the U.S. and its territories and possessions under the conditions specified in C.1. below. Except as specified in B.2. below, referral through Program S is the only means by which eligible spouses will receive preference for positions filled through competitive procedures in the commuting area of the sponsor's permanent duty station.

2. This Chapter DOES NOT apply to positions described below. However, Components and/or activities should establish procedures to ensure that eligible spouses have an opportunity to apply and receive proper consideration for positions covered in 2.a. through 2.e.

a. Positions in the excepted service;

b. Positions filled from Office of Personnel Management certificates or under agency Delegated Examining Unit or Direct Hire Authority procedures;

c. Nonappropriated fund (NAF) positions;

d. Positions in foreign areas, whether in the competitive or excepted service;

e. Positions filled under Component career program procedures, in which case the Components must establish procedures for the consideration of spouse preference eligibles;

f. Positions filled at the full performance level that are covered by a mandatory mobility agreement;

g. Positions in the Defense Civilian Intelligence Personnel System and those in organizations that have as a primary function intelligence, counterintelligence, or national security;

h. Positions filled through noncompetitive procedures; or

i. Any DoD position for which a spouse applies or is referred after the spouse has already obtained Federal employment in an appropriated or nonappropriated fund continuing position within the commuting area of the sponsor's duty station.

3. **Continuing and Non-Continuing Positions**

a. Military spouse preference applies to both continuing and non-continuing positions. Continuing positions are those to which appointments are made without time limitation and which have fixed full-time or part-time work schedules. Non-continuing positions include:

(1) Positions filled by temporary or term appointment, including NAF time-limited appointments, regardless of duration or work schedule;

(2) Positions filled by permanent appointment with intermittent work schedules; and

(3) NAF positions with a "flexible" work schedule, or any NAF position for which the employment category is identified as "flexible."

b. There is no limit to the number of times military spouse preference may be applied for non-continuing positions. Provided they meet all other eligibility requirements, spouses retain preference for continuing and non-continuing positions until acceptance or declination of a continuing position as explained in Section C.4. below. Declination of a non-continuing position has no effect on eligibility for other non-continuing positions. The following special procedures apply to spouses who accept non-continuing positions:

(1) If a spouse accepts a temporary or term appointment, including a NAF time-limited appointment, of more than 60 days, the registering HRO must amend the Program S registration by entering "N" (Not Available) in the "TEMPORARY" data element. Eligibility for subsequent time-limited appointments is suspended until 60 days prior to the expiration of the temporary or term appointment. At that time, the spouse may request re-registration for time-limited employment. If the duration of the appointment is 60 days or less, eligibility for other non-continuing positions is not suspended. In this case, the "TEMPORARY" data element on the registration should be changed to "N" only at the request of the spouse.

(2) Accepting a permanent appointment to a position with an intermittent work

schedule, including a permanent NAF position with a flexible employment category or work schedule, has no effect on continued eligibility for other non-continuing positions.

C. REGISTRATION ELIGIBILITY

1. **Basic Requirements**. Registration in Program S is limited to spouses of active duty military members of the U.S. Armed Forces (including the U.S. Coast Guard and full-time National Guard). Also, except as specified in C.1.f. below, the spouse may register only if he or she accompanies a military sponsor who is:

a. Assigned by a Permanent Change of Station (PCS) move from overseas to U.S., or to a different commuting area within the U.S., including the U.S. territories or possessions;

b. Relocating to a new and permanent duty station after completing basic and advanced individual training;

c. Permanently assigned to the same duty station where initial entry training was received;

d. Assigned by PCS to a service school regardless of the duration of training;

e. A former military member who re-enlists and is placed directly in a permanent assignment; or

f. Reassigned on an unaccompanied tour by PCS with orders specifying the sequential assignment, except when the sequential assignment is in the same commuting area from which the sponsor was reassigned. Once the spouse has actually established a residence and relocated to the commuting area of the sponsor's sequential assignment, he or she may register for activities in that area if otherwise eligible. As an alternative, spouses may register in Program S before joining the sponsor at the sequential permanent duty station, but not earlier than 30 days prior to the sponsor's reporting date. Spouses may only use this alternative if they are relocating to join their sponsors at the sequential duty station on or before the sponsor's reporting date.

2. **Other Requirements**. In addition to meeting the requirements in C.1. above, all of the following conditions must be met.

a. For spouses whose only eligibility is under the E.O. 13473 appointing authority, the marriage to the sponsor must have occurred on, or prior to, the date of the military sponsor's orders authorizing the PCS or amended orders authorizing the spouse to travel as a dependent. For spouses whose eligibility is based on another valid noncompetitive appointing authority or interchange agreement, the marriage to the sponsor must have occurred prior to the sponsor's reporting date to the new duty station.

b. The spouse must meet all pre-employment criteria and be eligible for immediate noncompetitive appointment to a position in the competitive service. Spouses who are eligible under more than one appointing authority may register using either authority. Unless eligible under another valid noncompetitive appointing authority or interchange agreement, spouses serving on VRA appointments and Schedule A appointments for the disabled are eligible only while still employed.

c. The spouse must furnish copies of the following to the registering activity.

(1) PCS orders identifying the date of issuance and the sponsor's reporting date:

(2) A current narrative resume (see Chapter 3, Section B.3.);

(3) The most recent performance appraisal: and

(4) Documentation of Executive Order (EO) 12721 or EO 13473 eligibility, if applicable, as prescribed in Parts 315.608 and 315.612, respectively, of reference (c); and

(5) A completed SF-75, "Request for Preliminary Employment Data," if applicable.

(6) Documentation of Leave Without Pay (LWOP), if applicable.

3. **Relocation for Purposes of Retirement or Separation**. Spouses are not eligible for Program S when their sponsor relocates in conjunction with retirement or separation.

4. **Termination of Eligibility**. Eligibility for Program S terminates upon:

a. Acceptance or declination of a continuing position in the Federal service in the commuting area of the sponsor's new permanent duty station, including a NAF position (includes positions in the military exchange services), whether or not preference was applied and regardless of whether the job offer would be considered valid for PPP purposes.

b. Refusal to participate in established competitive recruitment procedures (e.g., interview, responding to KSAs, etc.);

c. Loss of spousal status due to divorce, death of the sponsor, or sponsor's retirement or separation from active duty; or

d. Failure to maintain immediate appointability as required by Section C.2.b. above.

5. **Automatic Termination of Registration**. Program S registration is automatically terminated 12 months after initial registration or the last extension or file maintenance action. Prior to such termination, both the spouse and the registering activity are notified as specified in E.6. below. Spouses whose registrations are automatically terminated may re-

register if still otherwise eligible.

D. <u>REGISTRATION OPTIONS</u>

1. A spouse may register at the losing A-coded activity up to 30 calendar days prior to the sponsor's reporting date or, upon relocation, at any A-coded activity in the commuting area of the sponsor's new duty station. Spouses who register with E.O. 13473 eligibility may use the 30-day option, but they cannot be appointed until they have relocated with the military sponsor to the new duty station. If the sponsor's PCS orders specify a "Not later Than" (NLT) reporting date, and the sponsor will be reporting prior to the NLT date, the spouse may register up to 30 calendar days prior to the actual reporting date. However, the spouse must present a written statement from the sponsor's gaining organization confirming the actual reporting date. Spouses who do not initially relocate with their sponsors cannot register until they are actually residing in the commuting area of the new duty station. The spouse must carry a completed SF-75, "Request for Preliminary Employment Data" or equivalent, to the A-coded activity in the new area.

2. An otherwise eligible spouse who is not currently employed by the Department of Defense may register at an A-coded activity in the gaining area or, if registration is desired in advance, at any A-coded activity in the losing area.

3. If the spouse is registered prior to the PCS move, the registering HRO must counsel the spouse to register at an A-coded activity in the new commuting area upon arrival. The A-coded activity in the new commuting area must verify the spouse's eligibility and then complete a new registration to change the activity code, address, telephone number and any other data that needs revision. The Priority Placement Support Branch (PPSB) then issues a notice to inform the "old" activity that the "new" activity has picked up the registration servicing.

4. DoD employees who are also military spouses have the following registration options if adversely affected by reduction-in-force (RIF), or by declination of transfer of function (TOF) or management-directed reassignment:

a. Registration under this Chapter, using their military spouse preference;

b. Registration in Program A using their displacement priority, in accordance with the procedures in Chapter 3 that normally apply to displaced employees; or,

c. Registration in Program A using their displacement priority for the commuting area of their sponsor's new duty location, effective only after arrival at the new location and only if otherwise still eligible. This option is not available unless, prior to the spouse's departure from the previous duty station, early PPP registration had been authorized, specific RIF notices had been issued, or the spouse had submitted written declination of a TOF out of the commuting area or written declination of a management-directed reassignment covered under Chapter 3, Section B.1.b.(7). Military spouses displaced while employed overseas may only use this option within the commuting area of their sponsor's overseas duty station.

E. REGISTERING ACTIVITY PROCEDURES

1. When registering a spouse in Program S, obtain a narrative resume, most recent performance appraisal, and a copy of the sponsor's orders. When the registering activity is being changed, the spouse should also provide a completed SF-75, or equivalent.

2. The registration should be completed in accordance with Program A procedures except as follows:

   a. **Program**. Enter "S"

   b. **Separation/Effective and Release Dates**. Leave blank. Registrations that are not extended by the HRO in accordance with the procedures in Section E.6. below automatically expire 1 year after registration or the most recent file maintenance, whichever is later.

   c. **Overseas Country**. Enter overseas country location code if spouse is returning from overseas; otherwise leave blank.

   d. **Priority**. Enter "S".

   e. **Return Rights**. Enter "N" if an entry was made in the "Overseas Country" Data Element; otherwise leave blank.

   f. **Return Rights AK-HI-RQ-GQ**. If the new duty station of the sponsor is Alaska (AK), Hawaii (HI), Puerto Rico (RQ), or Guam (GQ) enter the corresponding code.

   g. **Skills**. Program S registrants must meet the established minimum qualification standards for all occupational series and grades for which registered. They are not subject to the standard PPP well-qualified criterion. Spouses registering with EO 13473 eligibility may register for the highest grade for which basically qualified down to the lowest grade for which they are available. Spouses registering on the basis of other noncompetitive appointing authorities may register for the highest grade previously held on a permanent basis down to the lowest grade for which they are available. Unlike registrants in all other PPP programs, military spouses registering in Program S are NOT required to register for their current skill.

   h. **Employee Information/Special Qualifications**. Enter the activity code of the losing activity.

   i. **Area of Referral**. Limit registration to activities within the commuting area of the sponsor's permanent duty station or, if the spouse is eligible under Section C.1.f. above, the commuting area of the sponsor's sequential assignment. The spouse may elect to

Page reissued 8/1/2012
Change memo H-FY2012-02

register for some or all of the activities in the commuting area without regard to Chapter 3, Section H, which prohibits "skipping over" activities.

3. Spouses must be counseled regarding:

a. Their option to delay registration until arrival at the new geographic location;

b. The rules on qualification requirements, salary and pay, and the conditions under which entitlement to spouse preference is terminated;

c. Their option of declaring availability for temporary, part-time, and intermittent employment, as well as the possible outcome of such a decision;

d. The importance of keeping registration data current, especially since failure to do so may lead to a loss of consideration; and

e. The requirement to comply with established recruitment procedures and be among the "best qualified" in order for preference to be applied for positions being filled competitively. Also, spouses should be advised that refusal to participate in the competitive process terminates preference.

4. When a spouse elects to register prior to accompanying the sponsor to the new duty station, the registering activity shall not effect the registration more than 30 days prior to the sponsor's reporting date or more than 30 days prior to the spouse's arrival in the new commuting area, whichever is later.

5. Narrative resumes and performance appraisals should be provided to gaining activities upon request.

6. **Extending Registration**. Registering human resource offices (HROs) and individual registrants are notified by the ASARS Daily Report (R11) 11 months after registration or the last file maintenance. Registrants are notified by mail from the Priority Placement Support Branch. For extending the registration, the HRO should review the data to verify continued eligibility and update registration Data Elements as necessary. Any completed file maintenance action extends the registration for 1 year. However, if no changes in registration data are submitted during the year, the registration must be extended by selecting the 30 Day Notices menu item from the ASARS main menu. This option may only be used within 30 days prior to the scheduled release from Program S.

7. **Change in Registering Activity**. To change the registering activity of an active Program S registrant, a new registration must be input. Once the new registration is submitted, the system generates a Report Action 31 to close out the old registration, and a notice is sent to the old registering activity on Daily Report (R13).

F. GAINING ACTIVITY PROCEDURES.

1. Eligible Program S registrants must be considered as military spouse preference candidates when referred through Program S for positions being filled through competitive procedures. They are eligible for spouse preference if they rank among the best qualified (BQ). As defined in Volume 315 of reference (b), a BQ military spouse possesses knowledge, skills, abilities, and competencies comparable to others who meet the competitive referral criteria for the specific position. Except as stipulated in Sections F.2. through F.4. below, and provided that all Priority 1 and 2 resumes have been cleared, a BQ military spouse blocks the selection of other competitive candidates. When more than one BQ military spouse is referred, selection from the group may be made in any order. Activities filling positions through competitive procedures must:

a. Requisition using Referral Code "S," "A," or "U" (see Chapter 8) and consider all spouses referred through Program S by the closing date of the announcement or, when certification is from existing registers or computerized referral lists, by an equivalent documented date. All other resumes received before and after the "closing" date must be cleared in accordance with standard procedures before the position can be committed;

b. Request a narrative resume and performance appraisal from the registering activity for each eligible military spouse; and

c. Rate and rank military spouses along with other candidates each time they are referred through Program S for consideration under competitive procedures. This is required even for spouses who were determined not BQ on prior referrals.

2. Program S referrals do not preclude the activity from filling a position using noncompetitive recruitment procedures. For the purposes of this Chapter, all candidates who are evaluated using a merit promotion crediting plan or other competitive screening factors are considered competitive candidates. The following examples illustrate the relationship between recruitment procedures and the applicability of military spouse preference.

a. An activity issues a competitive announcement, and the area of consideration includes reinstatement, reassignment, and change to lower grade eligibles. All applicants, including those who could be assigned to the position noncompetitively, are evaluated against standard competitive rating criteria. Fifteen BQ candidates are referred to the selecting official on a single referral list, and the list includes a military spouse who was referred through Program S. The selecting official wants to select a noncompetitive reassignment candidate from the competitive list. Even though the reassignment candidate could be placed noncompetitively, the recruitment procedures are considered to be competitive because all applicants were rated against competitive criteria. Therefore, the BQ military spouse blocks the selection of any of the other candidates on the list.

b. An activity issues a competitive announcement that includes noncompetitive reassignment eligibles in the area of consideration, but only the competitive candidates are evaluated using the rating and ranking criteria. A military spouse is referred through Program S and is ranked in the BQ category. The selecting official wants to offer the position to a noncompetitive reassignment candidate. Since the HRO did not rate and rank the non-competitive applicants with the competitive applicants, the selecting official can select the reassignment candidate without regard to the BQ spouse.

3. Military spouse preference does not apply if granting preference would:

    a. Result in the change to lower grade or separation of a current permanent, term, or temporary DoD employee of the activity;

    b. Violate statutes or regulations governing veterans' preference or nepotism; or

    c. Adversely affect programs for the achievement of minority and gender equality, programs for persons with disabilities, or programs for the affirmative employment of veterans.

4. Military spouses with less than 6 months remaining in the area may be nonselected for permanent continuing positions.

5. Gaining activities have final responsibility for verifying eligibility for spouse preference prior to appointment.

6. When a military spouse cannot be located by the registering activity after reasonable efforts have been made, the potential gaining activity may continue the staffing action without further consideration of that registrant. Such action, however, does not terminate the spouse's preference. Report Action Code 26 with a narrative explanation must be submitted and documentation must be maintained to provide a proper audit trail.

7. **Interviews**.

    a. Military spouses are subject to the same rating, ranking, and evaluation criteria used to assess other competitive candidates. Therefore, if personal interviews are being used as a competitive selection tool, BQ spouses may be interviewed as an exception to Chapter 4, Section D.1.c., which prohibits anyone representing the gaining activity from contacting a PPP registrant directly. However, the HRO must advise the selecting official that a BQ military spouse eligible who is within reach for selection may not be passed over to select a non-spouse candidate, unless;

    (1) Spouse preference is not applicable as stipulated in Section F.3. above;

    (2) Selection is not mandatory as stipulated in Section F.4. above; or

    (3) A selection is made using noncompetitive procedures as stipulated in Section F.2. above.

b. As explained in Section C.4.b. above, spouses who refuse to be interviewed under these circumstances lose their preference and are no longer eligible for Program S.

➡ c. Military spouses are required to complete any assessment questionnaires that are required of other applicants in order for HROs to determine if they are BQ for the position. ⬅

G. COMPONENT EXCEPTIONS

As stipulated in Volume 315 of reference (b), heads of DoD Components may establish guidelines for approving exceptions to spouse preference procedures. Exceptions shall be rare and based only on compelling hardship to the Component or the applicant. This authority may be delegated within the Component.

➡

CHAPTER 14

APPENDIX A

PROGRAM S REGISTRATION/COUNSELING CHECKLIST

INSTRUCTIONS: Initial the blank to the left of each applicable item and indicate responses by circling the appropriate options. Items with an asterisk (*) correspond with data elements on the PPP Registration Format. Your initials acknowledge that your Registration Format corresponds with the circled options.

Registrant's Name: _____

GENERAL ACKNOWLEDGMENT

1._____ I understand that the DoD Military Spouse Preference Program (Program S of the PPP), applies to positions that are being filled through competitive procedures except those listed in the next two items.

2._____ I understand that Program S does not apply to positions filled from Office of Personnel Management (OPM) certificates; through delegated examining or direct hire authorities granted by OPM; or through Component career programs. I also understand Program S does not apply to excepted service positions; positions in foreign overseas areas; Non-Appropriated Fund (NAF) positions; or educator positions within the DoD Dependents' Schools system. In order to exercise military spouse preference for such positions, I must apply in accordance with established application or self-nomination procedures.

3._____ I understand that neither military spouse preference nor Program S applies to positions covered by the Defense Civilian Intelligence Personnel System (DCIPS) or to positions in DoD organizations that have as a primary function the areas of intelligence, or counterintelligence.

4._____ I understand my sponsor must be an *active* duty military member of the U.S. Armed Forces (including the U.S. Coast Guard and full-time National Guard or Reserves), and I must be immediately appointable to a position in the competitive Federal service.

5._____ I understand that spouse preference and Program S do not apply to positions outside the commuting area of my sponsor's permanent duty station.

APPOINTMENT ELIGIBILITY

(If multiple options apply, check only the appointing authority preferred by the registrant.)

6._____ Current career or career-conditional employee

7._____ Currently serving on a Veterans Recruitment Authority (VRA) appointment

8._____ Eligible as non-competitive reinstatement candidate

9._____ Eligible under Executive Order 12721 (expires 3 yrs. after return to U.S.)

10._____ Eligible under Executive Order 13473 and accompanying sponsor on a PCS move with orders dated after our marriage (expires 2 yrs after date of sponsor's orders for each PCS)

11._____ Eligible under an interchange agreement

SKILLS: SERIES AND GRADES

13._____ I understand I must meet the established minimum qualification standards for all occupational series and grades for which registered. I also understand the highest grade for which I may register will be determined in accordance with the appointing authority upon which registration is based, but I may register for the lowest grade acceptable to me.

AVAILABILITY

14._____ I am (**available / not available**) for time-limited employment. I understand that if I accept or decline such an offer, I will remain in the PPP for permanent and other time-limited appointments. I also understand that if I accept a time-limited appointment (including NAF) of more than 60 days, the registering HR Office must amend the Program S registration by entering "N" (Not Available) in the "TEMPORARY" data element. Eligibility for subsequent time-limited appointments is suspended until 60 days prior to the expiration of the temporary or term appointment. At that time, I may request re-registration for time-limited employment. If the duration of the appointment is 60 days or less, eligibility for other non-continuing positions is not suspended.

15._____ I am available for (circle Yes or No) : **Part Time:** Yes / No; **Intermittent:** Yes / No; **Seasonal:** Yes / No; **Rotating Shifts:** Yes / No. I understand that a permanent appointment with a part-time, seasonal, or rotating-shift work schedule meets the definition of a "continuing position" for purposes of spouse preference (see #24 below).

16._____ I am (**available / not available**) for supervisory positions.

17._____ I am (**eligible / not eligible**) for Defense Acquisition positions. If I meet the DAWIA qualification requirements, I will provide the necessary documentation to the registering HRO.

18._____ I am (**available / not available**) for referral to <u>closure</u> activities.

19._____ (If appropriate) I have been counseled regarding registration for (check applicable items):

    a._____ WG-0000 - General Wage Grade, WG-1 thru WG-4 (except series 5703, 3105, & 3111)

    b._____ WG-01111 - Trades Helper, WG-5 only (excludes series in Chapter 7, App. F)

    c._____ GS-300 - General Clerical & Administrative Support, GS-1 thru GS-4, with or without STC/OAA/DAT (does not cover GS-675, GS-679, GS-1702 or GS-2091)

GENERAL POLICY/PROCEDURES

20._____ I understand that if I am registering within 30 days of my PCS to my sponsor's new duty station, upon relocation I must report to the new duty station HR Office to update my registration. If I fail to report within 30 days, my registration will be deleted.

21._____ The definition of a "continuing position" has been explained to me. I understand that I am eligible for only one offer of a continuing position, and if I receive such an offer I am expected to accept or decline within 2 business days.

22._____ I understand that I must keep the HR Office informed of my whereabouts so they can contact me regarding job offers. Failure to keep the HR Office informed may lead to removal from the PPP.

23._____ I understand if I accept or decline a continuing position in the Federal service, including a NAF position (includes positions in the military exchange services), my Program S registration will be terminated, whether or not preference was applied. This applies to positions I apply for on my own initiative, not just positions offered through the PPP.

24._____I understand my spouse preference terminates if I refuse to participate in established competitive recruitment procedures (e.g., submitting an application, being interviewed, etc.).

25._____I understand my Program S registration will be terminated upon loss of spousal status due to divorce, death of the sponsor, or the sponsor's retirement or separation from active duty, and that I am responsible for notifying the registering HRO of any changes that may affect my eligibility.

26._____I understand my Program S registration will be terminated upon expiration of the authority upon which registration is based (e.g., E.O. 12721, E.O. 13473, VRA, etc.).

27._____ I understand that Chapter 3, Section B.3, and Chapter 14, Section E, of the PPP Handbook require me to submit a complete, current and accurate resume in order to register in the PPP.

OTHER INFORMATION

28._____ The Social Security Number entered on my registration form is correct.

29._____ I (**am / am not**) on workers' compensation or light duty.

30._____ I have not had performance or conduct problems within the last 12 months.

Registrant's Signature   **Date**

Counselor's Signature   **Date**
(Note: Counselor's signature also certifies that the spouse's current/last official rating of record, if applicable, is at least fully satisfactory/successful or Level 3 or above on a 5-point scale)

DOCUMENTS PROVIDED

_____ Narrative resume

_____ PCS orders (Must show reporting date, local duty station and indicate authorized family member movement) or amended orders adding spouse as an authorized dependent

_____ SF-50s (e.g., LWOP, highest grade held, overseas appointments, etc., if applicable)

_____ SF-75 (if applicable)

_____ Documentation of performance rating of record (if applicable)

_____ Other (e.g., marriage license, verification of overseas employment, etc., if applicable; also documentation of LWOP, if applicable, when SF-50 is not available)

PRIVACY ACT STATEMENT: Sections 1301, 3302, 3502 of Title 5, U.S. Code provide for the issuance of rules governing solicitation of this information. Gaining and releasing activities use this information to place registrants, report actions and update data as well as refer names to potential employers or to provide information to you about potential employment. Furnishing the requested information is voluntary, but failure to provide it may result in missed opportunity for placement or reemployment under the respective placement assistance program.

E.O. 9397 authorizes use of the Social Security Number (SSN) as the means of identifying individuals in personnel information systems to provide placement assistance. Your SSN will only be used to ensure accurate program registration. Furnishing your SSN is voluntary, but failure to do so may result in not obtaining placement consideration.

Index

A
Accomplishments, 16
Administrative jobs
    DOD poasitions, 43
    non-DOD positions, 44
    sample positions, 43, 44
    sample resumes for, 49–52, 56–61, 89–90, 94–97
Advanced leave, 12
Annual leave, 12
Applications
    Derived Preference, 93
    ideas for standing out, 47
    for non-DOD jobs, 44
    on USAJOBS, 43, 46

B
Best Qualified ratings, 47

C
Childbirth, 12
Childcare, 12
Classification standards, 15
Compensatory time off, 12
Competitive Service jobs, 8, 72–73, 80
    eligibility for, 72, 73
    on USAJOBS, 72, 73
Confidentiality, 12
CORE Program Services Specialists: example Excepted Service
  positions, 81

D
Deceased veterans
    mothers of, 92
    spouses of, 23, 92
Department of Defense (DOD)
    Military Spouse Preference program. *See* Program S
    Priority Placement Program (PPP), 20, *See also* Program S

sample jobs, 43

sample results email from, 93

Dependent Care Flexible Spending Accounts (FSAs), 7, 12

Derived Preference, 92

application with, 93

eligibility for, 92

employment benefits, 8

grade levels, 10

sample resume for, 94–97

Disabled veterans

mothers of, 92

spouses of, 10, 23, 92

Documents, 36

match notifications, 42, 48

sample results email, 93

sample welcome email, 37

USAJOBS, 77, 78

what to bring to Program S meetings, 38

Donated leave, 12

E

Education

GS grade levels based on, 11

what to include in your federal resume, 18

Elder care, 12

Emails

match notifications, 42, 48

results, 93

welcome, 37

Employee Assistance Program (EAP), 12

Excepted Service jobs, 8, 80

example positions, 81

sample resumes, 82

Executive Order (E.O.) 13473, 21, 23

F

Family and Medical Leave Act (FMLA), 12

Federal Emergency Management Agency (FEMA): example Excepted Service positions, 81

Federal Employees Retirement System (FERS), 7

Federal jobs, 7–18, 24

applying for, 43, 44, 46, 47

classification standards, 15

Competitive Service, 8, 72–73, 80

★ ★ ★ ★ ★ ★

Derived Preference, 8, 10
DOD positions, 43
employment benefits, 8, 10, 86
Excepted Service, 8, 80, 81
finding positions, 9
grade levels, 10
health insurance benefits, 7, 13
keywords for, 33–35
match notifications, 42
merit promotion positions, 8, 71–78, 72–73
NAF jobs, 8, 84–85, 86
negotiating for, 11
non-DOD positions, 44
position descriptions, 15
promotion potential, 11
retirement benefits, 7, 13
sample positions, 43, 44
searching for, 45
starting benefits, 10
on USAJOBS, 71–78
work-life benefits, 12
Federal long-term care insurance, 7
Federal resumes, 16, 26
case studies, 28–32, 48–54, 56–61, 67–69
competitive, 16
format for, 17
length of, 16
Outline Format, 16, 17, 74–76
samples, 74–76, 82, 94–97
what to include, 18
Federal salaries, 11
GS table, 14
salary levels, 11
Flexible Spending Accounts (FSAs), 7
Flexible work schedules, 12
Follow up, 46
Foreign language teachers: example Excepted Service positions, 81

*G*eneral Schedule (GS)
grade levels, 10
grade levels based on education alone, 11
salary table, 14

H

Health Care Flexible Spending Accounts (FSAs), 7
Health insurance, 7, 13
Human Resources jobs: sample resumes for, 49–52, 89–90
Human Resources Offices
    Program S contacts, 39
    sample welcome email from, 37

I

Insurance, 7, 13
Interviews, 47

J

Job announcements (samples), 73
Job applications
    Derived Preference, 93
    ideas for standing out, 47
    for non-DOD jobs, 44
    on USAJOBS.gov, 43, 46

K

Keywords for Option Codes, 33–35

L

Leave options, 12
Life insurance, 7
Long-term care insurance, 7

M

Marine Corps Community Services (MCCS): sample NAF jobs, 85
Match notifications, 42
    sample emails, 42, 48
Medical leave, 12
Meetings, 38
Merit promotion positions, 8, 73
    eligibility for, 72, 73
    on USAJOBS, 72, 73
Military Spouse Preference program, 23
Milton, Susanne (example), 94–97, 98–99
Morris, Jennifer (case study), 48–54, 89–90
Mothers, 92
Moves: Permanent Change of Station (PCS) orders, 23, 25

N

NAF jobs. *See* Non-appropriated fund jobs
Narrative resumes (case studies), 48–54, 55–65
National Defense Authorization Act (NDAA), 21
Negotiating, 11
Non-Appropriated Fund (NAF) jobs, 8, 84–85
    employment benefits, 86
    flexible positions, 86
    regular positions, 86
    retirement benefits, 86
    sample jobs, 84–85
Non-Appropriated Fund (NAF) resumes, 87–88
    requirements for, 87–88
    sample, 89–90

O

OCHR service centers
    Program S contacts, 39
    sample welcome email from, 37
Office of Personnel Management (OPM): classification standards, 15
Option Codes (Program S), 26, 100
    case study, 27
    keywords for, 33–35
Other qualifications, 18

P

Permanent Change of Station (PCS) orders, 23
    sample orders, 25
Personal information, 18
PPP. *See* Priority Placement Program
Pregnancy/childbirth, 12
Priority Placement Program (PPP), 20
    Program S, 8, 19–70, 100
    Team Program Coordinators, 39
Program management: sample resumes for, 56–61
Program S (Priority Placement Program), 19–70
    benefits for military spouses, 8
    case studies, 27, 41, 48–54, 55–65
    documents for, 36
    eligibility for, 21–23
    eligibility questionnaire, 40
    E.O. 13473 requirements for, 23
    handbook, 100

how it works, 20
HRO contacts for, 39
match notification, 42
meetings, 38
Option Codes, 26
registration, 36, 41
sample resumes, 49–52, 56–61, 67–69
STARS for, 20
ways to improve your registration, 41
Promotion potential, 11
Public Affairs Specialists (case study), 66–70

Q

Qualifications, 18

R

Resume Builder, 16
Resumes. *See also* Federal resumes
big block format, 62–65
bulleted format, 53–54, 70, 98–99
case studies, 48–54, 55–65
NAF requirements, 87–88
PPP-S narrative resumes, 48–54, 55–65
samples, 53–54, 62–65, 98–99
USAJOBS Resume Builder, 77
Retirement, 7, 13, 86
Richardson, Natalie (case study), 66–70
Robbins, Bobbi (case study), 27
job matches, 43
Option Codes, 27
Program S registration, 27, 41
resume, 28–32
Romeo, Lori-Anne (case study), 55–65

S

Salary
federal salaries, 11
GS salary table, 14
Sick leave, 12
Social Security, 7
Social workers: sample resume for, 82
Superior Qualifications Letters, 11

★ ★ ★ ★ ★ ★

T

Telework, 12
Troutman, Kathryn, 5

U

United States Air Force
    NAF resume requirements, 87–88
    sample NAF jobs, 85
United States Army
    NAF position benefits, 86
    sample Excepted Service positions, 81
    sample NAF jobs, 85
United States Marine Corps
    sample NAF jobs, 85
    sample PCS orders, 25
United States Navy: sample NAF jobs, 84, 85
USAJOBS, 9
    applying for jobs on, 43
    Competitive Service positions on, 72, 73
    documents for, 36
    follow up on, 46
    merit promotion positions on, 72
    Resume Builder, 16
    resumes in, 77
    sample resumes for, 56–61, 67–69, 94–97
    saved jobs, 78
    saved searches, 45, 78
    searching for job matches on, 45
    tips for, 78
USAJOBS Resume Builder, 77

V

Veterans: grade levels for, 10

W

Welcome emails, 37
Widows/widowers
    eligibility for Derived Preference, 92
    eligibility for Program S, 23
Work experience, 18
Work-life benefits, 12
Work schedules, 12

About the Author: Kathryn Troutman

1. Founder, President, and Manager of The Resume Place®, the first federal job search consulting and federal resume writing service in the world, and the producer of www.resume-place.com, the first website devoted to federal resume writing.

2. Pioneer designer of the federal resume format in 1995 with the publication of the leading resource for federal human resources and jobseekers worldwide—the *Federal Resume Guidebook*, now in its sixth edition.

3. Developer of the Ten Steps to a Federal Job®, a licensed curriculum and turnkey training program taught by more than 2,000 Certified Federal Job Search Trainers™ (CFJST) around the world.

4. Leading Federal Resume Writing, KSA, Resumix, ECQ and Federal Interview government contracted trainer. GSA Schedule Holder.

5. Author of numerous federal career publications (in addition to the *Federal Resume Guidebook* mentioned above):

The *Military to Federal Career Guide* is the first book for military personnel and is now in its second edition, featuring veteran federal resumes. Troutman recognized the need for returning military personnel from Iraq, Afghanistan, and Kosovo to have a resource available to them in their searches for government jobs.

Ten Steps to a Federal Job was published two months after 9/11 and was written for private industry jobseekers seeking first-time positions in the federal government, where they could contribute to our nation's security. Now in its third edition.

The *Jobseeker's Guide* started initially as the companion course handout to the *Ten Steps* book, but captured its own following when it became the handout text used by over 200 military installations throughout the world for transitioning military and family members. Now in its eighth edition.

With the looming human capital crisis and baby boomers retiring in government, the *Student's Federal Career Guide* was co-authored with Kathryn's daughter and MPP graduate, Emily Troutman, and is the first book for students pursuing a federal job. Now in its third edition, including the latest information on the changing structure of student programs, plus additional guidance for veterans taking advantage of the Post-9/11 GI Bill.

Resumes for Dummies by Joyce Lain Kennedy is renowned as the premier guidebook for resume writing. Kathryn and The Resume Place staff served as designers and producers of all the private industry resume samples for the fifth edition.

The Stars Are Lined Up for Military Spouses
TRAINING RESOURCES AND HELP FOR MILITARY SPOUSES!

MILITARY SPOUSE FEDERAL RESUME WRITING

The Resume Place, Inc. Federal Resume Writing services for Military Spouses. Professional consulting services, writing, editing, coaching services for military spouses to navigate Program S and USAJOBS applications. Federal Career Consulting on USAJOBS announcement selection and total federal job search services.

Request quotes and information: complete the Free Request Quote Form: www.resume-place.com

LICENSED CURRICULUM/ CERTIFICATION TRAINING:

This book and the Stars are Lined Up for Military Spouses Slide Deck are part of the Certified Federal Job Search® and Certified Federal Career Coach® curriculum. Get Certified and Licensed to teach Ten Steps to a Federal Job® and The Stars are Lined Up for Military Spouses at your military installation.

More information: http://www.fedjobtraining.com/certification-programs.htm

HALF-DAY WORKSHOP

The Stars Are Lined Up for Military Spouses is a 1/2 day course that is available to be taught at government agencies and military bases worldwide. The course is listed on the GSA Schedule and is available for your military base.

More information and requests for quotes: Kathryn Troutman, kathryn@resume-place.com

Publications by The Resume Place, Inc.

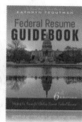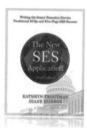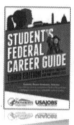

Order online at www.fedjobtraining.com | Bulk Orders: (888) 480 8265
FREE SHIPPING of bulk orders in the domestic US and APO; shipping is calculated
for HI and overseas

EBooks Available for Immediate Download

Many of our titles are available in PDF or Kindle versions for immediate download when ordered from our site.

Jobseeker's Guide, 8th Edition

Military to Federal Career Transition Resource Workbook and guide for the Ten Steps to a Federal Job® training curriculum. Federal job search strategies for first-time jobseekers who are separating military and family members. *$18.95 ea., Bulk Rates Available*

The Stars Are Lined Up for Military Spouses

Federal Jobs for Mliitary Spouses through USAJOBS, Program S, NAF and Excepted Service Key book to assist military spouses with navigating the complex federal job process. Covers four ways to land the major kinds of federal positions for military spouses.
$14.95 ea., Bulk Rates Available

Federal Resume Guidebook, 6th Ed.

Now the #2 Resume Book in America! The ultimate guide in federal resume and KSA writing. Easy to use as a template for writing. Specialty occupational series chapters. *$15.95 ea., Bulk Rates Available*

The New SES Application, 2nd Ed.

The SES job application is complex. The New SES Application breaks it down into a step-by-step process based on a popular workshop taught for over 10 years. Plus, the book has updated the SES info to help you navigate hiring reforms currently impacting the Senior Executive Service. *$21.95 ea., Bulk Rates Available*

Student's Federal Career Guide, 3rd Ed.

3rd Edition takes the 2013 IndieFab Gold Winner for Career Books! Outstanding book for jobseekers who are just getting out of college and whose education will help the applicant get qualified for a position. 20 samples of recent graduate resumes with emphasis on college degrees, courses, major papers, internships, and relevant work experiences. Outstanding usability of samples on the CD-ROM.
$9.95 ea., print copies sold out; available in PDF

Creating Your First Resume

Creating Your First Resume is a book that will be used at high school and technical school programs nationwide. The new edition boasts brand new resume samples that represent the push toward STEM technical programs to provide training and certifications for high school students. *$12.95 ea., Bulk Rates Available*

Ten Steps to a Federal Job, 3rd Ed.

Written for a first-time applicant, particularly those making a career change from private industry to federal government. Case studies include 24 before & after successful resumes! *$18.95 ea., Bulk Rates Available*

Online Federal Resume Database

This Online Federal Resume Database contains more than 110 resume samples and federal job search resources from the current Resume Place publications. Each CD-ROM has a clearly organized interface. Sample resumes are available in Word and PDF format for quick previewing and easy editing. *Individual and Agency / Base Licenses Available*